Spiritual Quest

The Institute of Ismaili Studies

OCCASIONAL PAPERS, 3

1. *The Poetics of Religious Experience: The Islamic Context* by Aziz Esmail
2. *Mysticism and the Plurality of Meaning: The Case of the Ismailis of Rural Iran* by Rafique Keshavjee

Spiritual Quest

Reflections on Qur'ānic Prayer According to the Teachings of Imam 'Alī

REZA SHAH-KAZEMI

I.B.Tauris *Publishers*
LONDON • NEW YORK
in association with
The Institute of Ismaili Studies
London, 2011

Published in 2011 and reprinted in 2014 by I.B.Tauris & Co. Ltd
6 Salem Road, London W2 4BU
175 Fifth Avenue, New York, NY 10010
www.ibtauris.com

in association with The Institute of Ismaili Studies
210 Euston Road, London NW1 2DA
www.iis.ac.uk

Distributed in the United States and Canada Exclusively by Palgrave Macmillan,
175 Fifth Avenue, New York, NY 10010

ISBN: 978 1 84885 447 5

A full CIP record for this book is available from the British Library
A full CIP record for this book is available from the Library of Congress

Library of Congress catalog card: available

Typeset in Minion Tra for The Institute of Ismaili Studies
Printed and bound in Great Britain by TJ International Ltd, Padstow, Cornwall

The Institute of Ismaili Studies

The Institute of Ismaili Studies was established in 1977 with the object of promoting scholarship and learning on Islam, in the historical as well as contemporary contexts, and a better understanding of its relationship with other societies and faiths.

The Institute's programmes encourage a perspective which is not confined to the theological and religious heritage of Islam, but seeks to explore the relationship of religious ideas to broader dimensions of society and culture. The programmes thus encourage an interdisciplinary approach to the materials of Islamic history and thought. Particular attention is also given to issues of modernity that arise as Muslims seek to relate their heritage to the contemporary situation.

Within the Islamic tradition, the Institute's programmes promote research on those areas which have, to date, received relatively little attention from scholars. These include the intellectual and literary expressions of Shiʿism in general, and Ismailism in particular.

In the context of Islamic societies, the Institute's programmes are informed by the full range and diversity of cultures in which Islam is practised today, from the Middle East, South and Central Asia, and Africa to the industrialised societies of the West, thus taking into consideration the variety of contexts which shape the ideals, beliefs and practices of the faith.

These objectives are realised through concrete programmes and activities organised and implemented by various departments of the Institute. The Institute also collaborates periodically, on a programme-specific basis, with other institutions of learning in the United Kingdom and abroad.

The Institute's academic publications fall into a number of interrelated categories:

1. Occasional papers or essays addressing broad themes of the relationship between religion and society, with special reference to Islam.
2. Monographs exploring specific aspects of Islamic faith and culture, or the contributions of individual Muslim thinkers or writers.
3. Editions or translations of significant primary or secondary texts.
4. Translations of poetic or literary texts which illustrate the rich heritage of spiritual, devotional and symbolic expressions in Muslim history.
5. Works on Ismaili history and thought, and the relationship of the Ismailis to other traditions, communities and schools of thought in Islam.
6. Proceedings of conferences and seminars sponsored by the Institute.
7. Bibliographical works and catalogues which document manuscripts, printed texts and other source materials.

This book falls into category one listed above.

In facilitating these and other publications, the Institute's sole aim is to encourage original research and analysis of relevant issues. While every effort is made to ensure that the publications are of a high academic standard, there is naturally bound to be a diversity of views, ideas and interpretations. As such, the opinions expressed in these publications must be understood as belonging to their authors alone.

Contents

Introduction

> There is no benefit in recitation without contemplation;
> there is no benefit in worship without comprehension.
>
> Imam ʿAlī[1]

Universal Significance and Contemporary Relevance

The Qurʾān describes itself in one of its verses as a 'clarification of everything' (*tibyānan li-kulli shay*'; 16:89). This implies that the scope of the guidance found in the Qurʾān cannot be restricted to any particular time or place; it must contain, not a blueprint for each and every situation that might arise in any time or place, but a set of guiding principles which are universally valid and can thus be applied appropriately in any time or place. The universal significance of the Qurʾān therefore strictly implies its contemporary relevance, and this relevance can be brought to light only by a creative interpretive engagement with the revealed text. Rather than uncritically regurgitating the literal meaning of the verses, and imagining that they can in and of themselves provide 'clarification' of everything, Muslims are called upon to ponder thoughtfully the principles embodied in the verses, and to use their intelligence to arrive at solutions—moral, intellectual and spiritual—to the complex issues generated by ever-changing conditions. In other words, *taqlīd*, or simple 'imitation', is to give way to *taḥqīq*, personal 'verification', in the quest for meaning. Such a quest for personal verification, in relation to the meaning of the Qurʾān, cannot dispense with established traditional principles of commentary, needless to say. But neither can the quest for personal meaning be satisfied by merely studying the interpretations of one's predecessors, however compelling they may be. Muslims of all major schools of thought are encouraged to engage with the Qurʾānic revelation creatively, intelligently and sensitively; Qurʾānic prayer will then be accompanied and deepened by both rational comprehension and intuitive understanding. This all-embracing intellectual engagement enhances receptivity to the sacramental presence of the revealed Word (*kalām*)—and thus to the theurgic power granted by the Speaker (*al-Mutakallim*) of that Word.

This monograph offers some reflections on certain chapters of the Qurʾān which are recited by Muslims in their daily prayers (*al-ṣalāt*; in Persian, *namāz*). I begin with a discussion of the opening chapter of the Qurʾān, *al-Fātiḥa*, which is the very foundation of the daily prayers, the closest equivalent in Islam to the *Pater Noster* ('Our Father') in Christianity. Then I reflect upon some of the chapters of the Qurʾān recommended for prayer within the broadly defined Shiʿi tradition—encompassing the Jaʿfari, Ismaili, Zaydi and Bohra branches of Shiʿi Islam. The attention given to these short chapters does not in any way imply a confessional prejudice on my part. These chapters are recited by all Muslims, Sunni and Shiʿi, but my remit here is to focus on the depth of meaning which can be discerned in those chapters specifically recommended for prayer within the Shiʿi traditions of Islam.

There is nothing exclusive about the list of chapters given here: Muslims of all schools of thought and praxis recite these chapters, either in the course of their canonical daily prayers, optional prayers, or as part of a litany or in their personal supplications. The sole difference between Sunni and Shiʿi practice in regard to recitation within the formal canonical prayer is that Sunni Muslims are free to recite any verse or set of verses or chapters, whereas Shiʿi Muslims are enjoined to recite only entire chapters in their prayers. The reflections offered here, therefore, are not intended to pertain only to Shiʿi Islam; rather they are intended to give some idea of the kind of spiritual, intellectual and ethical dynamics with which all Muslims engage, to one degree or another, when they recite and meditate upon the chapters of the Qurʾān presented here.

The universality aimed at here pertains not only to all denominations within Islam; it also concerns the temporal dimension, that is, we are concerned with quintessential principles of spirituality which, being timeless, apply just as much today as they did at the time of the revelation of the Qurʾān. Moreover, the very nature of the Qurʾānic message transcends religious boundaries, delivering a message of wisdom which unites rather than divides: the basic message of *tawḥīd*—not just 'Oneness' but 'declaring One', 'affirming One', and at the deepest level, 'realising One'—cannot be restricted to the formal framework of Islam. Rather, it resonates with all those whose quest for meaning and fulfilment is rooted in faith—that is, in faith as such, and not only such and such a faith. As I hope to show in the reflections which follow, one of the central themes of the Qur'ānic discourse is the affirmation of religious diversity in the very bosom of spiritual unity—a theme which needs to be stressed more than ever in our troubled times.[2]

Moreover, the Qur'ānic message reaches out beyond even religious boundaries, with its repeated insistence upon the unity of humanity: 'Your creation and your resurrection [O mankind] are but as [the creation and resurrection of] a single soul' (31:28). This essential unity of the human race derives from the God-given and inalterable nature of the human soul: 'So set thy purpose for religion with unswerving devotion—the nature [framed] of God (*fiṭrat Allāh*), according to which He hath created man. There is no altering God's creation. That is the right religion, but most people know not' (30:33). This primordial nature is the foundation upon which all truth and virtue, wisdom and holiness arise; following a particular religion is of value only insofar as it brings to fruition these spiritual seeds contained within the *fiṭra* of each and every human soul.

Reflection and Comprehension

I would like to make it clear that the reflections offered here do not constitute a formal commentary, in the manner of a traditional *tafsīr*. Such a task is quite beyond the competence of this writer, presupposing as it does mastery of a host of traditional sciences, for which formal training, under a range of teachers qualified in their respective disciplines, is essential. Rather, the intention here is far more modest: addressing a general readership, I aim to present a series of philosophical reflections, guided by exegetical principles drawn from the teachings of Imam 'Alī, while referring occasionally to traditional spiritual commentaries. The purpose is not to be comprehensive but illustrative: to illustrate some of the ways in which verses of the Qur'ān, when 'prayerfully' reflected upon, might be brought into sharper focus by means of an intellectual mode of reflection on the chapters and verses under discussion.

Such an approach might be considered as a personal response to the repeated Qur'ānic injunctions to reflect and meditate on the verses of the Qur'ān: 'God hath made clear unto you His verses [or: signs, *āyāt*] in order that ye might reflect' (2:219; repeated almost verbatim at 2:266). Or again: 'Truly, herein are signs for those who reflect' (13:3). The insistence of the Qur'ān upon *tafakkur*, reflection or meditation, is one of the most remarkable 'intellectual' features of this scripture: 17 verses contain an explicit or implict encouragement to engage in *tafakkur*.[3] There are several other key notions underscoring the need to engage intellectually with the Qur'ān, such as *tadabbur* (to ponder),[4] *tafaqquh* (to comprehend), *'aqila* (to use one's intellect), *ta'allum* (to learn), etc. To take the latter term alone: its root, *'-l-m* (to know), together with its derivatives, occurs no fewer than 856 times in the Qur'ān.[5]

In this light one appreciates more clearly Imam 'Alī's succinct statement on the relationship between action and contemplation, or outward worship and inward comprehension: 'There is no religion for one who has no intellect.'[6] The importance of prayer in the Islamic tradition, likewise, is summed up in one verse of the Qur'ān: *I created the jinn and mankind only that they might worship Me* (51:56).[7] The following sentence of Imam 'Alī can be read as a comment on this verse: 'I enjoin you to pray, for it is the pillar of religion and the foundation of Islam. So neglect it not.'[8] Neglecting the prayer means not only failing to pray, it also means praying in a mechanical fashion, paying lip-service to the prayers without making any effort to engage in meditative reflection upon what one is saying. The active processes of contemplation (*tadabbur*) and comprehension (*tafaqquh*)—the *tadabbur* and *tafaqquh* mentioned in our opening citation above—are not regarded by Imam 'Alī as being confined to some elitist minority of 'thinkers' within the community; they are an intrinsic part of the performance of prayer, without which prayer itself is truncated or emasculated—deprived of its full efficacy. Therefore every Muslim who prays, and not just the 'contemplatives', should engage in meditative reflection as an essential component of the prayer. Without this effort of thought, only the *ẓāhir*, or 'outwardly apparent' meaning, will be discerned; the Imam urges each Muslim not to remain content at this level, but to penetrate into the depths of meaning, the *bāṭin*, or 'inwardly hidden', doing so by means of that mode of esoteric interpretation, *ta'wīl*, for which he was renowned. The Prophet said that while he had to struggle to establish the *tanzīl*, 'descent' or 'revelation', of the Qur'ān, Imam 'Alī was the one who would have to struggle for its *ta'wīl*.[9] Indeed, throughout the history of Islamic spirituality, Sunni and Shiʿi alike, Imam ʿAlī is cited as the companion most renowned for his stress on meditation of the verses of the revelation.

Al-Ghazālī, for example, cites the following saying of the Imam: 'There is no good in a devotional act that is not understood, nor in Qurʾān reading that is not pondered over.'[10] Another saying of the Imam's, cited by al-Ghazālī, alludes to the unlimited scope of knowledge that can be attained through deep meditation on the meanings embedded in the depths of the Qurʾānic verses: 'One who understands the Qurʾān can thereby explain the totality of knowledge.'[11] He also said, famously: 'The Qurʾān consists of a book inscribed, between two covers; it speaks not with a tongue, it cannot do without an interpreter (*tarjumān*).'[12] That he saw himself as the interpreter par excellence of the Qurʾān, following the death of the Prophet, is made clear in several sayings. For example, he claimed to be 'the speaking Qurʾān (*al-Qur'ān al-nāṭiq*)' for the community when his opponents at the battle of Ṣiffīn called for the Qur'ān to be used as the basis of arbitration.[13] He also claimed to be able to load 70 camels with the pages of the commentary he could give on the *Fātiḥa*.[14] The foundational role of Imam ʿAlī in the formation of the discipline of scriptural exegesis in Islam is undisputed, both in Shiʿi and Sunni traditions of Islam; Ibn ʿAbbās, often referrred to in Sunni sources as the founding father of the science of exegesis, claimed that he learnt this discipline from Imam ʿAlī.[15]

The voluminous sayings attributed to Imam ʿAlī in respect of the exalted status of the intellect bear impressive testimony to the intellectual thrust which animates the heart of the ʿAlīd tradition: the Imam's knowledge, however vast and authoritative it may be, is intended to be a stimulus for individual intellectual creativity, not a substitute for it. 'The Truth cannot be known through others: know the Truth, and then will you come to know who are its people (*ahl*).'[16] Rather than accepting what a person says merely on account of his authority, one is urged to critically evaluate what the person says, to verify it for oneself: 'Consider not who said it, rather, consider what he said.'[17]

Sacred Presence

For Muslims, the Qur'ān is not just a book containing teachings, narratives, injunctions and prohibitions. It is indeed regarded as comprising all of these elements, but it is also grasped as something infinitely transcending them: it is deemed to be both revealed truth, explicitly articulated through words, and sacred presence, mysteriously conveyed by the divine Word. It is this element of presence which bestows upon all the other *informative* aspects of the text a dimension of *transformative* power. This helps to explain why it is that Muslims maintain that the Qur'ān is untranslatable, as well as having the quality of 'inimitability' (*iʿjāz*). What can be translated, to some degree of accuracy or another, is the literal meaning or semantic content of the text; but what cannot be translated is the element of *presence*—conveyed by the Word of God which is spoken in 'clear Arabic (*ʿArabī mubīn*)' (16:103; 26:195): 'We verily have established it as an Arabic Qur'ān . . .' (43:3).[18] It also helps to explain why the canonical prayer, *ṣalāt*, cannot be recited except in Arabic: the sacramental efficacy of *ṣalāt* in Islam is inextricably woven into the very texture of the Arabic language of the Qur'ānic Revelation.[19] While it is permissible—and indeed recommended—to express personal supplications (*duʿā'*) in one's own language, the formal *ṣalāt* is valid only if it be Qur'ānic in verbal form, as well as spiritual substance: the prayers must be drawn from the Qur'ān and uttered verbatim, in the original language of the Revelation.

There is therefore a balance, a synthesis and a complementarity between the element of revealed truth—the doctrinal content of the text—and the element of sacred presence. Without making an attempt to comprehend the truths of the Revelation, the sacred presence of the text will make only an existential impact, and therefore remain in large part unintelligible on the doctrinal plane. But without the element of presence, the 'truth' of the doctrines, the didactic narratives and the legal precepts will not go beyond the purely conceptual plane. When truth is joined to presence, however, these teachings make an impact on the soul which is both intellectual and existential: their meaning penetrates not just the intelligence but also the very heart and soul of the receptive listener/reciter. The whole being of one who is attuned to the divine 'music' of the Qur'ān is opened up to the spiritual power of the Revelation—the theurgic power unleashed by an inimitable symbiosis of sensible sound and intelligible light: sonoral presence of the sacred and enlightening exposition of the truth.

Seyyed Hossein Nasr sums up well what the Qur'ān's truth and presence, form and substance, spirit and matter, mean for Muslims who are sensitive to the sacred:

> For Muslims, everything about the Qur'ān is sacred—its sound, the very words of the Arabic language chosen by God to express His message, the letters in which it is written, and even the parchment and paper that constitutes the physical aspect of the sacred text. Muslims carry the Qur'ān with full awareness of its sacred reality and usually do not touch it unless they have made their ablutions and are ritually clean. They kiss it and pass under it when going on a journey, and many carry small copies of it with them at all times for protection. The Qur'ān is that central sacred presence which determines all aspects of Muslim life, and the source and fountainhead of all that can be authentically called Islamic.[20]

It is on account of the importance of the aspect of *presence*, conveyed through sound, that so much emphasis is placed by the Prophet and the Imams of his Ahl al-Bayt ('People of the House' or 'family') on reciting the Qur'ān beautifully. The Prophet said that among the greatest of the beauties of creation is 'the fine intonation of a beautiful voice (*naghmata'l-ṣawt al-ḥasan*)'.[21] He also said: 'Everything possesses its own adornment (*ḥilya*); and the adornment of the Qur'ān is a beautiful voice.'[22] Such was the beauty of the Qur'ānic recitation of Imam Zayn al-ʿĀbidīn ('Alī b. Ḥusayn) that, according to various reports, those hearing his recitation would 'swoon away due to the beauty of his voice (*ṣaʿiqa min ḥusni ṣawtihi*)'.[23] It should not be thought that it is only the aesthetic effect of the beautiful recitation that so deeply struck those who heard it; rather, it is the alchemical combination of enchanting musicality, profound meaning, and above all, theurgic power, that results in the soul being overwhelmed and possibly intoxicated by the divine Word.[24]

The Qur'ān refers to the unimaginable immensity of its own celestial 'gravity': if the Qur'ān were to descend upon a mountain, it would be 'humbled in awe and rent asunder by the fear of God' (59:21). The effect of this revelational descent upon a mountain might be compared with the effect of the self-manifestation (*tajallī*) of the divinity as such, as the following dialogue between God and Moses demonstrates. It is interesting to note that the same word (*ṣa'iqa*) which was used to describe how the listeners of the Imam Zayn al-'Ābidīn fell into a swoon is used here to describe how Moses was thunderstruck by the theophany he experienced. Moses asks to see God. The reply comes: 'Thou wilt not see Me, but look upon the mountain. If it stand still in its place, then thou wilt see Me. And when his Lord revealed Himself to the mountain, He caused it to collapse. And Moses fell down unconscious' (7:143).

Revelation as Self-Disclosure

The concept of *tajallī*—the theophany, self-revelation, self-manifestation or self-disclosure of God—takes us to the heart of the transformative power of the Qur'ān. It is a concept strongly associated with the principle of light, its root meaning being 'making evident', 'bringing to light', as the following verse makes clear: 'By the day when it shineth forth (*wa'l-nahāri idhā tajallā*)' (92:2). Just as God describes Himself as 'the Light of the heavens and the earth' (24:35), so the Qur'ān refers to itself as 'a manifest light' (4:174); 'a light from God' (5:15); and the biblical scriptures preceding it are referred to as 'guidance and light' (5:44 and 5:46). Since there is only one light—that of God, who is 'the Light of the Heavens and the earth'—it follows that the light of the Qur'ān can only be a prolongation of the Light of God. This light is associated with, but not reducible to, the principle of 'guidance'. This formal mode of guidance, rather, is itself an aspect of the light, so that one becomes 'enlightened' by the Qur'ān not just through its teachings but also by its luminosity. The light of the Revelation is that by which one 'sees' the Truth, and also that by means of which one comes to understand it. Spiritual vision, however, transcends comprehension, in the very measure that realised wisdom transcends conceptual knowledge: 'Eyes see Him not through sight's observation', said Imam

ʿAlī in one of his most renowned utterances, 'but hearts see Him through the verities of faith (*lā tudrikuhu'l-ʿuyūn bi-mushāhadati'l-ʿīyān, wa lākin tudrikuhu'l-qulūb bi-ḥaqā'iq al-īmān*)'.[25]

Imam ʿAlī uses the concept of *tajallī* to emphasise the real presence of God conveyed by the Qur'ān, and shows thereby the extent of the error of regarding the Qur'ān as simply a text like other texts: 'He has revealed Himself to them [His creatures] in His Book (*fa-tajjalā lahum fī kitābihi*)'.[26] This simple affirmation can be read in conjunction with the statement that God has similarly revealed Himself to His creatures by means of His creatures (*mutajallī li-khalqihi bi-khalqihi*),[27] which implies that the Qur'ān is an encapsulation of the whole of creation.[28] The Qur'ān is thus concretely perceived—and not just abstractly conceived—as a sonoral and textual recapitulation of the entire cosmos, and the cosmos is perceived as the Qur'ān writ large. It is not just the entire cosmos and the Qur'ān, but also man, the Adamic substance, that constitute stages or screens whereupon God reveals Himself. The following remarkable lines of poetry by Imam ʿAlī reveal the subtle relationships between the human being, the cosmos, and the revealed scripture: 'You consider yourself to be an insignificant body, but within you is encapsulated the greatest universe; and you are the "the manifest book" (*al-Kitāb al-mubīn*), whose letters reveal what is hidden'.[29]

The following prophecy of the Imam is worth reflecting upon, as it stresses the indispensable role of the Qur'ān, taken as a whole, in the spiritual and intellectual lives of the Muslims:

> Certainly, a time will come upon you, after I have passed away, when nothing will be more hidden than the Truth (*al-Ḥaqq*), and nothing more manifest than falsehood (*al-bāṭil*) . . . the people of this age to come will consider nothing of less value than the correct recitation of the Qur'ān (*ḥaqq tilāwatihi*), and nothing of more value than distorting its text . . . The holders of the Book will cast it away, its memorisers will forget it . . . at this time the Qur'ān, and those who were true to it, will be among the people, and yet not among them; with them, and yet not with them . . . Nothing of the Qur'ān will remain except its name; people will know nothing of it except its script and letters . . .[30]

This prophecy of the time of ignorance to come can be read as a commentary on the following injunction of the Prophet. He was asked how his followers would be delivered when they would be plunged in the prophesied age of tribulation (*fitna*), and he replied, citing 41:41–42: 'The exalted Book of God, to which falsehood has no access, neither in front of it, nor behind it; [it is] a Revelation from the Wise, the Praised.'[31]

Just as Imam ʿAlī indicated the correspondence between the Qur'ān, the universe and man, so the Prophet alluded to an equally mysterious correspondence between the Qur'ān and the Imam: 'The Qur'ān is incumbent upon you, so take it as an *imām* and a leader (*qā'ida*).'[32] In this light, the meaning of the famous *ḥadīth al-thaqalayn* assumes a deeper significance: the Prophet said he was leaving behind as his heritage 'two weighty things (*thaqalayn*), the Book of God, and the people of my household (*ahl baytī*)'.[33] The Qur'ān is that which conveys most directly the presence, light and guidance of which the Imams of the Ahl al-Bayt are perfect embodiments. It is for this reason that Imam ʿAlī can refer to himself, as noted above, as the 'speaking Qur'ān'; and that the Prophet said: "Alī is with the Qur'ān and the Qur'ān is with ʿAlī. They will not separate from each other until they return to me at the [paradisal] pool (*al-ḥawḍ*).'[34] These sayings indicate a correspondence between the perfect *walī Allāh* and the revealed *kitāb Allāh*, the 'Friend' or saint of God, and the 'Book' of God, a correspondence which is made even more explicit by the Imam in the following saying, which we will use as the hermeneutical basis of our own reflections:

> The Book of God is that by means of which you see, speak and hear. Parts of it speak through other parts, and some parts of it bear witness to other parts (*yanṭiqu baʿḍuhu bi-baʿḍ, wa yashhadu baʿḍuhu ʿalā baʿḍ*).[35]

Taking this saying together with the previously cited one, according to which he himself is the 'speaking Qur'ān', one observes that Imam ʿAlī is claiming that he is one who sees, speaks and hears by means of the Qur'ān, and is inviting each of his followers to become like him, and not just be guided by the light, the presence and the meaning of the Qur'ān: rather, one is made aware of the possibility of becoming one with that light, presence and meaning. This leads us to observe the subtle relationship between assimilating the presence of the Qur'ān and entering into the sphere of *walāya* ('sanctity'); for this latter principle is described in a *ḥadīth qudsī* (a 'holy utterance' spoken by God, but transmitted by the Prophet) in terms which evoke Imam 'Alī's invitation to see, speak and hear through the Qur'ān.

> My slave draws near to Me through nothing I love more than that which I have made obligatory for him. My slave never ceases to draw near to Me through supererogatory acts until I love him. And when I love him, I am his hearing by which he hears, his sight by which he sees, his hand by which he grasps, and his foot by which he walks.[36]

There is, therefore, a correspondence between the realised saint, through whom God sees, hears, speaks and acts, on the one hand, and, on the other, the divine presence conveyed by the Qur'ān, through which, according to Imam 'Alī, one sees, speaks and hears: the holiness of *walāya* and the theophany of *tajallī* are both at work in the *walī Allāh*, and in the Qur'ānic Revelation; the 'two weighty things' are as one in their substance and in their transformative and enlightening function of rendering God present.

We find the Prophet saying: 'Whoever yearns for God should listen to the speech of God (*kalām Allāh*, i.e., the Qur'ān).'[37] The role of the recitation of the Qur'ān in view of spiritual realisation is of great importance. Imam 'Alī refers to this in the following sayings: 'Learn the Book of God, for it is the best of speech and the most eloquent exhortation. Meditate deeply upon it (*tafaqqahū fīhi*), for truly it is the spring of hearts; and seek to be cured by its light, for indeed it is "a remedy for what is in the hearts" [referring to 10:57].'[38] Also: 'In it [the Qur'ān] there is a cure for the greatest sickness, which is infidelity and hypocrisy, deviation and error.'[39]

At the highest level, the spiritual impact of the Qur'ān is described in terms of a process of infusing Prophethood into the soul: 'For one who recites the Qur'ān, it is as if Prophethood is being woven into his very being (*fa-ka'annamā udrijat al-nubuwwa bayn janbayhi*), except that he cannot be the recipient of the Revelation [i.e., cannot be regarded as a Prophet in the strict sense].'[40] This kind of statement can only be explained in terms of the immensity of the divine presence which is conveyed by the recitation of the divine discourse. The reciter is being penetrated by the divine presence, and for this reason it is *as if* he were being transformed into a Prophetic being; but only one who receives the Revelation directly and immediately from God is a Prophet in the full sense; all of those who receive the Revelation as mediated by the Prophet cannot therefore be qualified as Prophets, hence the phrase *ka'annamā*, 'as if'. This phrase comes again in a saying attributed to the Prophet: 'For one who recites a third of the Qur'ān, it is as if he were given a third of Prophethood; and he who recites two-thirds of the Qur'ān, it is as if he were given two-thirds of Prophethood; and he who recites the whole of the Qur'ān, it is as if he were given the whole of Prophethood.'[41]

Such is the realisational force proper to immersion in the divine Word that later mystics would assert, along with Abū Madyan (d.1198), the seminal Maghribi spiritual authority from whom many Sufi orders claim descent: 'The aspirant (*al-murīd*) is not a true aspirant until he finds in the Qur'ān everything to which he aspires.' This statement is cited by Ibn 'Arabī in his magnum opus, *al-Futūḥāt al-Makkiyya*, and in the same passage, he writes himself that when the Qur'ān truly 'descends' upon the heart, and not just the tongue, the result is a sweetness (*ḥalāwa*) beyond all measure, surpassing all delight (*ladhdha*).[42] As Martin Lings notes: 'The Sufis speak of "seeking to be drowned" (*istighrāq*) in the verses of the Qur'ān . . . What they are seeking is, to use another Sufi term, extinction (*fanā'*) of the created in the Uncreated, of the temporal in the Eternal, of the finite in the Infinite; and for some Sufis the recitation of the Qur'ān has been, throughout their life, their chief means of concentration upon God.'[43]

Finally, let us note the following saying of the Prophet, which brings together two key spiritual or methodical principles, namely, intensity of prayer and the assimilation of the Qur'ān: 'The most noble of my community (*ashraf ummatī*) are the bearers of the Qur'ān, and those who keep vigil at night (*aṣḥāb al-layl*).'[44] One of the chief spiritual practices of the night vigil (*qiyām al-layl*) is, precisely, the recitation of the Qur'ān; the other being the invocation of the Name of God (*dhikr Allāh*). Both practices are mentioned in the following verses from the chapter entitled *al-Muzzammil* ('The Enwrapped'); these verses are among the most important as regards exhorting the Muslims to engage in nocturnal devotion. First, as regards the recitation:

> O thou enwrapped in thy cloak,
> Stand in prayer all night, save a little—
> A half thereof, or lessen it a little.
> Or add to it, and recite the Qur'ān in measured recitation (73:1–4).

Then, as regards the invocation:

> So invoke the Name of thy Lord and devote thyself to Him [or 'it', the 'Name'] with utter devotion (73:1–8).

* * *

The first chapter of this monograph will be devoted entirely to the *Fātiḥa*, the cornerstone of daily prayer in Islam. The second will then present, one after the other, the chapters which are most often recited by Shiʿi Muslims in their prayers, after having recited the *Fātiḥa*. The Shiʿi practice of reciting entire chapters is based on the precept inherited from the Shiʿi Imams, to which al-Qāḍī al-Nuʿmān, the leading Fatimid jurist and theologian, refers in his classical work, *Daʿāʾim al-Islām*: 'Begin each unit of prayer with the *Basmala* [the formula: *Bismi'Llāh al-Raḥmān al-Raḥīm*] and then recite the *Fātiḥa*. And in the first two units of every prayer, recite a chapter of the Qur'ān after the *Fātiḥa*.'[45] This means that, in practice, the shorter chapters, coming towards the end of the Qur'ān, are the ones recommended for recitation. As regards which chapters in particular are to be recited, considerable leeway is given to the individual to choose whichever he or she wishes. The following saying of Imam Jaʿfar, cited by al-Qāḍī al-Nuʿmān, indicates the extent of the flexibility granted to the individual on this issue: 'When you are praying by yourself, lengthen the prayer,[46] for verily it is worship; when you pray with the congregation, lighten it [that is, make it short] and pray with [for the sake of] the weakest of them . . . The Messenger of God's prayer was the most brief, although it was perfect.'[47] Al-Qāḍī al-Nuʿmān sums up the attitude towards the prayers: 'In this matter [which chapters are to be recited] there are no hard and fast rules.'[48] Nonetheless, some recommendations are given as regards which *Sūra*s ought to be recited, and the selection given in this essay represents a broad cross-section of those most commonly recited in the major schools of Shiʿism.

Al-Fātiḥa: The Opening[1]

[1:1] *In the Name of God, the Compassionate, the Merciful.*
[1:2] *Praise be to God, Lord of all the worlds;*
[1:3] *The Compassionate, the Merciful;*
[1:4] *King of the Day of Judgement.*
[1:5] *Thee alone we worship and from Thee alone we seek help;*
[1:6] *Guide us upon the straight path;*
[1:7] *The path of those whom Thou hast blessed; not the path of those who are subjected to anger, nor of those who go astray.*

The importance of this chapter is expressed by many sayings of the Prophet Muḥammad, for example: 'There is no prayer without the *Fātiḥa* (*lā ṣalāta illā bi-fātiḥati'l-kitāb*).'[2] It is referred to by a number of epithets, all of which express its crucial status as embodying the quintessence of the Qur'ānic Revelation: *Umm al-kitāb* ('Mother of the Book'), *al-Sab' al-mathānī* ('The Seven [verses] oft-repeated'), *al-Shifā'* ('The Healing'), *al-Asās* ('The Foundation'); *al-Ṣalāt* ('The Prayer'), *al-Kāfiya* ('The Sufficient'), *al-Kanz* ('The Treasure'), *al-Nūr* ('The Light'), to cite some of the most important.[3] In one saying of the Prophet, found in the canonical Sunni collection of Bukhārī, the *Fātiḥa* is described as being 'the most tremendous chapter in the Qur'ān (*a'ẓam al-suwar fi'l-Qur'ān*)'; the Prophet continued, referring to it also as 'the seven [verses] oft-repeated (*al-sab' al-mathānī*), the tremendous Qur'ān (*al-Qur'ān al-'aẓīm*), which I have been given.'[4] The implication in this statement is that the *Fātiḥa* is not just the 'most tremendous chapter in the Qur'ān', but also that somehow it *constitutes* the 'tremendous Qur'ān' itself. In the verse referring to the 'seven oft-repeated', we read: 'We have given thee seven of the oft-repeated [verses] and the tremendous Qur'ān' (15:87), the implication here being that the seven verses are distinct from, or at least, a distinct part of, the Qur'ān as a whole. In the *ḥadīth*, however, it appears as if there is an identification of the whole with the part, the Qur'ān being as it were synthesised within the *Fātiḥa*, the *Fātiḥa* thus being the quintessence of the Qur'ān.

This identification between the *Fātiḥa* and the Qur'ān is further reinforced by this esoteric saying of Imam 'Alī: 'Everything in the Qur'ān is in the *Fātiḥa*; everything in the *Fātiḥa* is in the [phrase] *Bismi'Llāh al-Raḥmān al-Raḥīm*; everything in *Bismi'Llāh al-Raḥmān al-Raḥīm* is in the [letter] *bā'*; everything in the *bā'* is in the dot [beneath it]: and I am the dot beneath the *bā'*.'[5]

Our reflections on the *Fātiḥa* can be guided by this remarkable saying. I shall leave aside the challenging arcane dimensions of the final three parts of this saying, which go beyond the purposes of this monograph, and focus on the first two parts only, asking how the whole of the Qur'ān can be found in the *Fātiḥa*, and how the *Fātiḥa* can be found in the *Basmala*.[6] For in making this assertion, it is as if Imam 'Alī is implicitly issuing an invitation to every single Muslim who recites the *Fātiḥa*: Do you see the way in which the *Fātiḥa* encapsulates the entire Qur'ān, and how it in turn is encapsulated within the *Basmala*? Can you exercise your faculties of reason, imagination, reflection and meditation such as to discern and discover in this short chapter of seven verses everything that is contained within the Qur'ān, with its 114 chapters, comprising over 6,000 verses? What follows is my attempt to demonstrate how the teachings of the Qur'ān might be said to be 'contained' within the *Fātiḥa*, the veritable cornerstone of prayer in Islam.

We can begin by considering the structure of the *Fātiḥa*, and then proceed with a closer look at the themes configured within this structure. The verses of the chapter can be conceived as so many rungs in a ladder descending from the divine to the human. We begin with the formula of consecration, the 'name' by which ultimate Reality discloses itself, *Allāh*, whose intrinsic nature is described as 'the Compassionate, the Merciful'; this Absolute is then declared to be Lord of all creation and King of the Day of Judgement; and we finish with the human being, defined in a tripartite fashion: those graced by God, those who experience wrath, and those who go astray. In between these two descriptions of the divine and the human, respectively, we have, at the middle of the ladder, the *contact* between the divine and the human: God alone is worshipped, and from Him help is sought, the substance of this help being guidance along the straight path. So, in terms of the simple structure of the chapter, three quintessential elements of the Qur'ānic teaching can be seen to be comprised in seed-form: a revelation of the nature of ultimate Reality; the possibilities inherent in the nature of man; and the worship which leavens the soul and brings to fruition, through divine grace, the seeds of salvation embedded within the human being. One might say that the 'whole' of the Qur'ān is summarised in these principles, as simple on the surface as they are profound in depth.

To probe this depth a little, let us enter into a more detailed exploration of the thematic trajectories established by the verses of the *Fātiḥa*, and see whether these themes can indeed be said to encompass the entirety of the Qur'ānic teaching. If Imam 'Alī declares that the whole of the Qur'ān is contained within the *Fātiḥa*, this means that the *Fātiḥa* must be a synthesis of the Qur'ān; and that, conversely, the Qur'ān is the differentiated, diversified articulation of the synthetic principles expressed by the *Fātiḥa*: the Qur'ān is the *Fātiḥa* exteriorised, the *Fātiḥa* is the Qur'ān interiorised.[7] For the Muslim who is attuned to the totality of the Qur'ān, therefore, each recitation of the *Fātiḥa* renders present—potentially, virtually or actually—the quintessence of everything that the Qur'ān teaches by way of revealed truth, and everything that it constitutes by way of sacred presence.

As regards sacred presence, one readily appreciates how the spirit of the entire Qur'ān is rendered present through the recitation of the *Fātiḥa*, for the Qur'ān's essential substance is one, that is, it is simple, not compound. Although outwardly or formally composed of sounds, words and letters, the sacred substance of Revelation is one and the same throughout the whole of the Qur'ān, transforming its outward multiplicity of form into a seamless unity of essence; the substance is unique, invariably the same from verse to verse, even if some verses are invested with more theurgic power and doctrinal profundity than others.[8] As regards the aspect of truth, however, and the specific doctrinal content of the text, one needs to enter into more concrete details, and to creatively apply the exegetical principle of Imam 'Alī noted earlier: 'Parts of it [the Qur'ān] speak through other parts, and some parts of it bear witness to other parts.'

Let us then look at each of the principal themes of the *Fātiḥa*, as they occur in the order of their appearance, and evaluate them according to the exegetical principle expressed in Imam 'Alī's saying.

In doing so, we will place great stress on the principle of *Raḥma*, which one might translate as 'loving mercy', for reasons which will become clear in a moment. This principle is the essential message of the *Basmala*, which in turn must be the essential message both of the *Fātiḥa* and the whole of the Qur'ān, according to the implications of Imam 'Alī's saying. In what follows, then, we hope to show how the principle of *Raḥma* operates as a kind of celestial spring, from which gushes the river of the *Fātiḥa*; and how this river of the *Fātiḥa* flows into, and comes to constitute, the ocean of the Qur'ān.[9] Everything in that ocean is already 'in' the river, which in turn is 'in' the spring. The water which flows from the spring to the ocean can here symbolise the flow of the Revealed discourse, which arises out of the unseen (*al-ghayb*), the eternally unknowable Essence, hidden in the deepest ground of Being.[10]

1. Ontology (verses 1–3)

In the Name of God, the Compassionate, the Merciful
Praise be to God, Lord of all the worlds;
The Compassionate, the Merciful.

The 'Name' is that by means of which a thing becomes known. In relation to God, the revelation of the name *Allāh* is that by means of which the utterly unknowable essence of absolute Reality makes itself known, or makes known that aspect of itself which is knowable. The relative has no access to the Absolute save by means of the self-manifestation of the Absolute—and the most direct of these manifestations or theophanies is the 'Name' of God. Knowledge of the absolute reality of God, and the relative nature of all else, is implied by the second verse: *Praise be to God, Lord of all the worlds*. Praise belongs to God on principle, for everything else in existence depends upon the Lord for its very existence, from moment to moment, and not just as regards its initial creation: 'There is no thing which does not glorify Him with praise' (17:44). The 'praise' which every single thing offers God is constituted by its very existence, and everything that it does in consequence of existing diversifies and articulates this inescapable mode of praise. In philosophical parlance, the praise of every being is constituted by its *contingency*: it is contingent or possible being (*mumkin al-wujūd*), as opposed to necessary being (*wājib al-wujūd*). Lest this principle be taken in too abstract a sense, verses such as the following complement this philosophical truth with poetic imagery, which invites us to enter into this principle through contemplative vision: '. . . everything that is in the heavens and the earth praiseth God—and the birds in flight: each knoweth its prayer and glorification' (24:41). The whole of creation is a hymn to the glory of the Creator.

In mystical parlance, the praise of every being is constituted by the fact that it is a *maẓhar*, a locus or theatre for the manifestation of the attributes of God: all manifestation cannot but 'praise' the source of its manifestation. The Lord, *al-Rabb*, is not just the Creator of the world, creating it and then being separate from it; rather, the Lord also continuously sustains[11] the process of universal manifestation, and this function of sustenance implies the perpetual and inalienable presence of the sustainer in that which is sustained. To say that God is perpetually present within creation means that the divine presence is inescapable throughout the entire realm of the cosmos, such that, 'Wherever ye turn, there is the Face of God' (2:115).

Certainly, there is nothing that is in any way comparable to God: 'There is nothing like unto Him' (42:11); this means that the human being is incapable of conceiving or meditating upon the Essence of God: 'God warns you of His Self' (3:28; and repeated at 3:30).[12] But this transcendence (*tanzīh*) of the divine, relating to the hidden, inner dimension of the Real, does not preclude other dimensions of God: 'He is the First and the Last, the Outward and the Inward' (57:3). The 'dimensions' of divinity designated by these four Names by no means exhaust the totality of the divine nature, which is expressed by the whole panoply of Names and Attributes referred to throughout the Qur'ān. The following passage contains the longest litany of divine Names:

> He is God, other than whom there is no divinity, the Knower of the invisible and the visible. He is the Compassionate, the Merciful. He is God, other than whom there is no divinity, the King, the Holy One, Peace, the Keeper of Faith, the Guardian, the Majestic, the Compeller, the Superb. Glorified be God from all that they ascribe as partner [unto Him]. He is God, the Creator, the Shaper out of naught, the Fashioner. His are the most beautiful Names. All that

> is in the heavens and the earth glorifieth Him; and He is the Mighty, the Wise (59:22–24).

In uttering the single name *Allāh*, then, all of the Names of God are implicitly invoked, and thus, an entire theology—in the exact sense of 'knowledge of God'—is summoned up and rendered present in essence. Taken together, these Names—and particularly 'the Outward' as the complement to 'the Inward'—imply that nothing is to be found in existence which is not a manifestation of one or more of the aspects of God. The verse mentioned above, 'wherever ye turn there is the Face of God', implies that this 'Face' of God which is everywhere 'visible' or 'apparent' (*al-Ẓāhir*) is mirrored by and within existent things which are its manifestations. However, as manifestations they are distinct from the Principle of which they are manifestations. All such manifestations of God remain, therefore, relative, and cannot be equated with God as such. On the one hand, the relativity of every manifest thing constitutes its 'praise' of the source of all manifestation; and on the other, it implies its own ineluctable transience, and hence nothingness, in the 'Face' of the Absolute: only that which is eternal is absolutely Real. 'Everything thereon is perishing; and there abideth [only] the Face of thy Lord, Owner of Majesty and Honour' (55:26–27).

These principles, expressing some of the deepest implications of *Tawḥīd*—the affirmation and, ultimately, realisation of the Oneness of God—are all evoked and thus, in a sense, encapsulated in the first and second verses of the *Fātiḥa*. One can see clearly here a shift from 'theological' *tawḥīd* (*al-tawḥīd al-ulūhī*) to 'ontological' *tawḥīd* (*al-tawḥīd al-wujūdī*), a transition which is one of the distinctive features of the writings of the 14th-century Persian mystic, Sayyid Ḥaydar Āmulī, one of the most important figures in the gnostic tradition of Shiʿi Islam.[13] He refers to the 'folk of the outward' (*ahl al-ẓāhir*) who pronounce the formula *Lā ilāha illa'Llāh* in the sense conveyed by the following Qur'ānic verse, an exclamation by the polytheists of the strangeness of the idea of affirming one God as opposed to many deities: 'Does he make the gods one God? This is a strange thing' (38:5). The monotheistic affirmation is, for Āmulī, the essence of the *tawḥīd* professed by the folk of the exterior, and is called 'theological' *tawḥīd* (*al-tawḥīd al-ulūhī*). In contrast, the 'folk of the inward' (*ahl al-bāṭin*) see through the multiplicity of created entities and affirm the sole reality of God whose oneness is not of the numerical order, but of an ontological nature; in the words of Imam ʿAlī to which we will return below: 'that which has no second does not enter the category of number'. It is from sayings such as these that the sages of both Shiʿi ʿIrfān and Sunni Sufism assert almost with one voice that 'there is nothing in existence apart from God (*laysa fī'l-wujūd siwa'Llāh*)',[14] and they cite the verse 'Everything is perishing save His Face' (28:88), among many others, in support of their comprehension of the principle of ontological *tawḥīd*. So, on the one hand, there is nothing which has authentic being except God's 'Face'; and on the other, this 'Face' is witnessed, wherever one turns. This means that the divine principle is both transcendent and immanent, absolutely inaccessible and yet mysteriously inescapable. On the one hand, as already cited: 'there is nothing like Him' (42:11); on the other, God is 'closer to man than his jugular vein' (50:16).

Returning to the first verse, the *Basmala*, it should be noted that the principles of mercy and compassion are integrated into the metaphysical affirmation of the absolute reality of God. For immediately after making God 'known' through His Name *Allāh*, the nature of this divine reality is described using two terms from the same root: *Raḥma*.[15] This term should be translated not only in terms of mercy and compassion—which do indeed constitute its immediate meaning—but also with the word 'love', as the following incident in the life of the Prophet makes clear. At the conquest of Mecca, certain captives were brought to the Prophet. There was a woman among them, running frantically and calling for her baby; she found him, held him to her breast and fed him. The Prophet said to his companions: 'Do you think this woman would cast her child into the fire?' We said, 'No, she could not do such a thing.' He said, 'God is more lovingly compassionate (*arḥam*) to His servants than is this woman to her child.'[16] Now, the *Raḥma* of God is here defined by reference to a quality which all can recognise immediately as *love*, rather than simply compassion or mercy. The mother will be compassionate towards her child, but this quality is derivative: compassion here derives from something more fundamental than mere sympathy or pity; rather, it streams forth from an overwhelming, irresistible, and as it were organic love which the mother has for her child.[17]

It is in this light that one can discern the significance of Allāh—a word simply meaning 'the divinity' or 'that which is worshipped'—being described immediately by two Names stressing *Raḥma*: God is the *lovingly* compassionate, the *lovingly* merciful. The Name *al-Raḥmān* is understood to refer to the power of creation, and *al-Raḥīm* to that of salvific redemption: love is thus the alpha and omega of existence. Given that the *Basmala* is the formula of consecration par excellence in Islam—initiating not just every legitimate act, but also every chapter in the Qur'ān but one[18]—its fundamental message is woven daily into not just the prayers but every aspect of the lives of Muslims. Being constantly invoked, the qualities of mercy and love are thus perpetually *evoked*: rendered present, active and transformative. These are the qualities which prevail over all else in the soul of the Muslim who is fully attuned to the Qur'ānic Revelation, and indeed, to the very nature of God. According to the Prophet, the words 'My Mercy prevails over My Wrath' are written by God 'in His Book, upon his very soul (*kataba fī kitābihi 'alā nafsihi*).'[19]

Given the fact that among the divine Names one also finds names which express the wrathful or rigorous side of God, such as 'The All-Conquering' (*al-Qahhār*), 'The Avenger' (*al-Muntaqim*), etc., it is of added significance that the formula of consecration contains a reiteration of the theme of loving mercy. One might have thought it more 'logical' or balanced, more in accordance with the 'scales' of divine justice, to include a name of rigour in so definitive a consecration. Thus, a formula such as: 'In the Name of God, the Compassionate, the Powerful' might be considered more appropriate. But the very fact that two Names of mercy are given in this formula which inaugurates the Revelation, and consecrates every act of significance for the Muslim, allows one to see that the essential nature of ultimate Reality is compassionate and merciful, these two attributes being expressive of the overflow of infinite love. 'I am as My slave thinks of Me', we are told in a profound *ḥadīth qudsī*.[20] The *Basmala*, by its very nature, encourages us to think of God as loving mercy. The truth of the first testimony (*shahāda*) of Islam is thus inextricably tied to the principle expressed by the *Basmala*: 'There is no god except Him, the Compassionate, the Merciful (*Lā ilāha illā Huwa al-Raḥmān al-Raḥīm*)' (2:163). The indubitable truth of *tawḥīd* is at one with the irresistible power of

Raḥma: 'our Lord is *al-Rāḥmān*, from whom we seek assistance against what you [disbelievers] allege' (21:112).

The reiteration of these two Names of Mercy in the *Basmala* and then in verse 3, helps us to see how it is that the principle of loving mercy permeates the message of the whole of the Qur'ān. The *Basmala*, as noted above, can be conceived as a 'spring' of loving mercy whence flows the 'river' of the *Fātiḥa*, and from which is formed the 'ocean' of the Qur'ān. In all three, it is the principles of mercy, compassion, peace and love which predominate over their opposites—wrath, vengeance, war and hatred. We say 'reiteration' and not 'repetition' of the Names of Mercy, for it is asserted in the exegetical tradition that there is no repetition as such in the Qur'ān: if something is said twice or more, it is so for the sake of stress, insistence, and emphasis, and is not to be deemed mere repetition, duplication or multiplication. What is being stressed in this instance, at the very outset of the *Fātiḥa*, and of the Qur'ān, is that God is inherently, essentially and overwhelmingly compassionate, merciful and loving. The quality of *Raḥma* is that which most fully evokes the essential nature of God. The entire message of the Qur'ān is thus one of *Raḥma*.

This principle is expressed throughout the Qur'ān in a multitude of ways. Perhaps the most important of these verses is the following: 'Call upon *Allāh* or call upon *al-Raḥmān*—whichever you call upon, unto Him belong the most beautiful Names' (17:110). Here we are informed of the intimate relationship between the reality of *Allāh* and the particular quality of *Raḥma* denoted by the Name *al-Raḥmān*. This particular quality, however, is also the most universal, the most all-embracing: 'My mercy encompasses all things' (7:156). It is also mercy, alone, among the divine Names and Attributes, that is 'prescribed' by God for Himself. The following verse reinforces the *ḥadīth* cited above, which tells us that God's mercy prevails over or precedes His anger: 'And when those who believe in Our revelations come to you, say, "Peace be with you", your Lord hath prescribed mercy for Himself' (6:54). This is repeated earlier in the same chapter, at 6:12: 'He hath prescribed mercy for Himself.' The Arabic here has the word *kataba*, 'he wrote', the implication being: God 'wrote' a law, thus making something incumbent upon Himself. One could also translate this phrase as 'He has made mercy incumbent upon Himself'; this image of writing a law for oneself can be seen as a graphic metaphor for expressing the metaphysical truth that mercy is 'inscribed' in the very nature of the divine Essence. No other attribute of God is described in this manner.

In chapter 55, entitled *al-Raḥmān* (described as the 'bride' [*'arūs*] of the Qur'ān by the Prophet), as well as in many other verses throughout the Qur'ān, it is made clear that *al-Raḥmān* is identified with the Creator. It is *al-Raḥmān* who 'created man', bestowing discernment and speech upon him (55:3-4), and who establishes the entire order and harmony of the heavens and the earth, summed up in the concept of 'the measure' or 'the equilibrium', *al-mīzān* (55:7–9). This implies that the quality of loving compassion proper to *al-Raḥmān* is infused not only into the fundamental equilibrium, harmony and rhythms of the cosmos, but also into all of the Names designating the creative function of God (such as *al-Khāliq*, the 'Creator'), *al-Bāri'* (the 'Shaper'), *al-Muṣawwir* (the 'Fashioner'), *al-Fāṭir* (the 'Originator'), among others. The creation stems from *Raḥma*, by virtue of the originating power of *al-Raḥman*, and returns to *Raḥma* by virtue of the saving power of *al-Raḥīm*: '. . . they cease not to differ, except those upon whom God has mercy: "*for this did He create them*"' (11:118–119; emphasis added). The initial *mīzān* or equilibrium established by *al-Raḥmān* is restored by *al-Raḥīm* after having been disturbed or ruptured by—or within—man. So when the Qur'ān tells us repeatedly that 'unto Him all things return', we are to understand that it is to this beatific love that all things are restored. If the *Basmala* initiates the Qur'ān, it is because *Raḥma* is the root of creation; and just as *Raḥma* initiates all things and encompasses all things, so it consummates all things. Mercy will have the last word, as the discussion on the theme of eschatology, in the following verse, will confirm.

We have noted that *Raḥma* can be viewed as the water of the spring of the *Basmala* and thus the substance of the river of the *Fātiḥa* and of the ocean of the Qur'ān. Let us join to this metaphor another, deriving from the root of the word *Raḥma* itself, the womb, *raḥim*: divine *Raḥma* can now be seen as the 'matrix'—understanding this word etymologically, from the Latin *mater*, meaning 'womb', 'mother'—which contains within itself the entire cosmos. The created realm is not just born from *Raḥma*, it is perpetually encompassed by it and nourished by it at every instant,[21] as the mother's womb nourishes and encompasses the embryo growing within it. The relationship between the maternal aspect of *raḥma* and the Prophet is highlighted by one of his epithets, *al-Nabī al-ummī*. His quality as *ummī* refers not only to the fact that he was 'unlettered', but also, taking this word literally, that he pertained to 'the mother', *al-umm*. According to the 15th-century Persian poet ʿAbd al-Raḥmān Jāmī, the Prophet was nourished by the *Umm al-Kitāb*, 'the Mother of the Book', therefore he must be seen as 'belonging to the mother, *umm*'.[22] It is also interesting to note that the Prophet's daughter, Fāṭima, was referred to as *Umm Abīhā* ('mother of her father')—which adds further resonance to the archetypal correspondences being considered here: Fāṭima symbolises the *Umm al-Kitāb*, from whom is 'born' or 'nourished' the 'unlettered' Prophet who 'belongs to the mother', *al-Nabī al-ummī*.[23]

In numerous narrations, the Prophet's character is likened to the Qurʾān.[24] The Qurʾān itself underscores in several verses the *Raḥma* which defines the essence of his character. In possibly the most direct and specific reference to the Prophetic substance as being pure mercy, the following verse proclaims unequivocally that the Prophet was sent by God *only* 'as a mercy to all of creation (*raḥmatan li'l-ʿālamīn*)' (21:107). One of the reasons for the success of the Prophet's mission, according to the Qurʾān, was the kind and merciful character of the Prophet; these qualities, together with gentleness, wise forbearance, patience, and magnanimity, constitute that *ḥilm*[25] for which he was indeed renowned, and to which all traditional accounts of his life and mission attest: 'It was by the mercy of God that thou wast gentle with them, for if thou hadst been harsh and hard-hearted they would have scattered from you' (3:159). Imam Jaʿfar al-Ṣādiq, commenting upon the verse, 'Whoever obeys the Messenger has obeyed God' (4:80), said: 'Between Himself and them [His creatures], He placed one of their own species, clothing him in His own attributes of compassion and mercy.'[26]

Before moving to the second theme of the *Fātiḥa*, let us take note of the esoteric correspondence established between the Prophet and the *Basmala*. At the very beginning of his Qurʾānic commentary, Kāshānī interprets the *Basmala* in such a way as to show the spiritual equivalence of the 'Name of God' (*ism Allāh*), and 'the perfect human form' (*al-ṣūra al-insāniyya al-kāmila*). For he says that the formula of consecration means esoterically: 'I begin to recite with the perfect human form, synthesising the universal and the particular dimensions of mercy—that perfect human form which is the locus for the manifestation (*maẓhar*) of the divine Essence and the ultimate Reality, comprising all Its Attributes.'[27]

The relationship between the *Basmala* and the Prophet, as being the 'Perfect Man' par excellence, is underlined by Kāshānī who cites the *ḥadīth*: 'I was granted the all-comprehensive words', adding by way of comment: 'for "the words" (*al-kalimāt*) are the spiritual realities and the [transcendent] sources of existing things'. He then refers to Jesus as 'a word (*kalima*) of God', in reference to 4:171. If in one respect the Prophet is akin to the Blessed Virgin in his receptivity to the Divine Word, in another, he is akin to Jesus as being identified with that Word himself. For Kāshānī identifies the supreme Word, that is, the Name of God, with the Prophet, doing so in his commentary on the verse in which God addresses the Prophet: 'So remember the Name of thy Lord . . . ' (73:8). Kāshānī interprets this Name to mean 'your own self'. He continues: 'that is, know yourself, and remember it . . . and strive to attain its perfections after having attained knowledge of its spiritual reality'.[28] This identification is made again in relation to verse 48:10: 'Truly those who swear allegiance to thee swear allegiance only to God. The Hand of God is above their hands . . .' Kāshānī comments: '*The Hand of God* is that which is manifested through the locus of manifestation constituted by His Messenger, who is His Greatest Name.'[29]

2. Eschatology (verse 4)

King of the Day of Judgement.

If this verse is read in the light of the previous ones, the notion of judgement will be seen to imply not only that each soul is accountable for its actions in the Hereafter, and will be recompensed accordingly, but also that the principle of justice according to which one will be judged is itself essentially fashioned by loving mercy. The *Raḥma* gushing forth from the preceding verses overflows into this verse, so that it comes to fashion the soul's fundamental attitude to the nature of the judgement it can expect in the Hereafter. Because of the predominance of compassion over anger in the divine nature, one articulates this call to 'the King' in an attitude of trust in a boundlessly merciful Lord, rather than in a state of terror in the face of an arbitrary dictator. The 'spiritual logic' of divine *Raḥma* implies, on the human plane, that our trust in mercy outweighs our fear of punishment—and this is the case, even if we have sinned. For we are told: 'O My slaves, ye who have been extravagant to the detriment of your souls, despair not of the mercy of God. Truly God forgiveth all sins; He is indeed the Forgiving, the Merciful' (39:53). And again: '. . . and who despaireth of the mercy of his Lord except those who are astray?' (15:56).

The clearest declaration that divine mercy puts an end even to the most grievous suffering brought about by the most evil acts is in the following *ḥadīth*. After the angels, the Prophets and the believers have all interceded for the sinners in hell, and those with neither the slightest good nor faith are alone left therein, God declares: 'The angels have interceded, the Prophets have interceded, and the believers have interceded, and none now remains save the Most Merciful of the Merciful (*arḥam al-rāḥimīn*).' God then takes a 'handful' from the Fire and casts them into a purifying river at the entrance to Paradise, which they enter.[30]

Another indication of the extent to which divine mercy defines the very Essence of the divine nature, and thereby determines the mode in which divine justice operates, is made clear in verses which tell us that the 'scales' of justice are weighted heavily in favour of mercy: 'Whoever cometh [before God] with a good deed will receive ten like it; but whoever cometh [before God] with an evil deed will only be requited with its like; and no injustice will be done to them' (6:160). This superabundant recompense of good, as opposed to a mere equivalence of recompense for evil, manifests clearly how much easier it is to fill the scales of good, making them 'heavy' with goodness, than to leave them 'light' and thus deprived of that celestial gravity which deepens one's receptivity to the grace of salvation and the 'beatific life' (*'īsha rāḍiya*) promised in the following verse: 'As for him whose scales are heavy, he shall live a beatific life' (101:7).

One of the clearest comments on the relationship between divine mercy and divine wrath is from a *ḥadīth qudsī* in which God declares: 'O son of Adam, so long as you call upon Me and ask of Me, I shall forgive what you have done, and I shall not mind. O son of Adam, were your sins to reach the clouds of the sky, and were you then to ask forgiveness of Me, I would forgive you.'[31]

All of the verses describing the Hereafter—the various levels and types of heavens and hells—can be seen as contained within this single reference to the 'King of the Day of Judgement', insofar as the principle of absolute justice referred to in symbolic terms of kingship is itself governed by the mercy proper to the divine nature, as expressed in the previous verses. This verse, then, together with the mercy invested in it, sheds light upon all of the references to the Hereafter, and places in proper context all wrathful acts ascribed to God in the Qur'ān. For it might be objected: if God is all-Merciful, what possible interest can He have in placing sinners in Hell forever? The answer can be given on two levels, one theological and the other mystical, but both derive their persuasive power from the mercy which is inherent to God and which is the leitmotif of the *Fātiḥa*—and, therefore, the whole of the Qur'ān, if one takes as axiomatic the saying of Imam ʿAlī that the whole of the Qur'ān is within the *Fātiḥa*, and the whole of the *Fātiḥa* is contained within the *Basmala*. Seen in this light, it is not surprising that Imam ʿAlī's definition of the true *faqīh* (literally 'one who understands') is 'he who never makes people despair of the *Raḥma* of God'.[32]

In theological terms, then, one observes the following argument, based on the distinction between a promise (*waʿd*) and a threat (*waʿīd*) in a saying of the Prophet: 'If God promises to recompense someone's act with a reward (*thawāb*), He will fulfill the promise (*Huwa munjiz lahu*), but when He threatens to punish an act, He is free to do what He wishes (*fa-Huwa fīhi bi'l-khiyār*).'[33] What this can imply, for those who are sensitive to the overriding reality of divine mercy, is that the hellish conditions depicted in the Qur'ān are not necessarily to be taken as literal descriptions of what is inevitably bound to occur; they can be read as descriptions of what *can* happen to the inveterate and unrepentant sinner. This theological position is upheld by, among other things, the following verses from the chapter named after Hūd, an Arabian Prophet: 'As for the wretched, they will be in the Fire; sighing and wailing will be their portion therein, abiding there for as long as the heavens and the earth endure—except as thy Lord willeth. Truly, thy Lord is doer of what He will' (11:106–107).

Two limitations on the time spent in Hell by the 'wretched' are to be noted here: on the one hand, 'for as long as the heavens and the earth endure'; and on the other, 'except as thy Lord willeth'. The final phrase, emphasising that God will do what He will (*fa"ālun limā yurīd*), can be understood to refer back to God's mercy, for what He 'wills' is in harmony with the inner law of mercy inscribed by Himself upon Himself. What He wills is what He is by nature, and He has described His nature as infinitely merciful.[34]

The mystical or Sufi answer to the question affirms this kind of theological reasoning, but normally goes further by stressing two factors: first, that if God's mercy encompasses all things, it must also finally encompass even Hell itself, and all suffering therein—thus no Hell or suffering can be 'eternal', God alone being eternal. Second, it is argued that God is not ultimately responsible for placing souls in Hell: each individual soul knows what it deserves, according to the principle of justice which will be made evident to it on the Day of Judgement: 'And We have tied every man's augury to his own neck, and We shall bring forth for him on the Day of Judgement a book which he will find open wide. [It will be said to him:] Read thy book. Thine own soul sufficeth this day unto thee as a reckoner' (17:13).

This verse can be read in conjunction with the following, 'Whatever good comes to you is from God, and whatever evil comes to you is from your own soul' (4:79). This makes it clear that goodness alone emanates from God to man; whatever else man experiences is solely the result of his own deeds, attitudes and dispositions. Hence, for the mystics, God's 'anger' is but a word describing the extrinsic consequence of a lack of receptivity on the part of man to the mercy of God.[35] These extrinsic consequences can indeed be terrible—neither posthumous suffering nor the hells are denied by the Sufis—but these consequences, labelled 'the wrath of God', are *contingent*, not essential; contingent in the sense of being called forth by contingent action—human sin—and thereby defined in terms of a disequilibrium which must be rectified. This takes us back to the notion of *al-mīzān*, the 'balance' or 'equilibrium' established by *al-Raḥmān*: all ruptures of this equilibrium must be rectified, and such rectification—morally referred to as the 'punishment' of God, mystically referred to as the inevitable consequences of a lack of receptivity to divine *Raḥma*—is itself an aspect of the mercy which encompasses all, for it is by means of this rectification that the sinner is enabled to return to God. The sinner abides in a hellish state unless he turns to God in repentance: 'save him who repenteth and believeth, and acteth virtuously; as for such, God will change their evil deeds to good deeds. God is ever Forgiving, Merciful' (25:69–70).

3. Worship (verse 5)

Thee alone we worship and from Thee alone we seek help.

In this verse we find summarised everything the Qur'ān teaches about prayer, the most essential point of contact between man and God. It expresses *tawḥīd* on the level of worship: nothing but God is adored, worshipped, supplicated, invoked. Practically each and every one of the verses of the Qur'ān which mention prayer, in any of its aspects, can be read as the starting point for trajectories of reflection which reveal how the principle of *tawḥīd* operates on this level of practical worship, and how it can be said that this integrating power proper to *tawḥīd* is perfectly articulated by verse 5 of the *Fātiḥa*. Let us take the following verse, 2:45, as the starting point for our reflections on this theme: 'Seek help [from God] through patient perseverance and prayer. And this is indeed hard, except for the humble.'

Humility is here given as the key to worship. In the absence of humility, worship will be a form of torture, for the proud person wishes to 'worship' nothing but himself; his own ego is the *de facto* 'god' whom he worships: 'Hast thou seen him who maketh his desire (*hawā*) his god?' (25:43; almost identical at 45:23). To worship God is not just an affront to the bloated self-esteem of the egotist, it is also a kind of death, for the egotist identifies so totally with his own ego that to depart from it in so absolute a manner as one does in worshipping and adoring God—the supreme Other as opposed to the glorified self—is tantamount to tearing the fabric of his very identity, woven as this is of selfish 'desire'. This state of affairs is summed up in verse 2:45, by stating how difficult it is for any but the humble to 'seek assistance' through patience and prayer. The humble soul finds in worship of God not only an ease, but also a sense of a homecoming, a return to the source of one's existence, and thus an infinite expansion and absolute enlivening of one's existence, not a death; for one's existence is no longer one's own, but is absorbed—in the deepest mode of contemplative prayer—within pure Being. The image of drops of water returning to the ocean whence they sprang is often given to allude to the simultaneous loss of particularity and gain of universality which takes place in this deepest kind of prayer. The gaining of universality is also understood in terms of the return to the root or principle of one's being, a reintegration within what the Qur'ān calls the *fiṭra*, the primordial, universal and unalterable nature of the human soul, as mentioned briefly earlier: 'So set thy purpose for religion with unswerving devotion—the nature [framed] of God (*fiṭrat Allāh*), according to which He hath created man. There is no altering God's creation. That is the right religion, but most people know not' (30:33).

Being true to one's deepest nature means to experience a longing for harmony with the source of one's existence, and this longing and yearning are most powerfully expressed in prayer. One yearns to have one's *fiṭra* perfectly conformed to *al-Fāṭir*, the 'Originator' of one's being, and to hear the words: 'O thou soul which art at peace, return unto thy Lord with gladness that is thine in Him and His in thee' (89:27–28).[36] This 'soul at peace' (*al-nafs al-muṭma'inna*) acquires its 'peace' through the remembrance of God: '. . . Those who believe and whose hearts are at peace in the remembrance of God—is it not in the remembrance of God that hearts are at peace?' (13:28). We shall be looking in more detail later at the various dimensions of *dhikr Allāh*; suffice to note here that this remembrance/invocation is described as being 'greater' (*akbar*) than the canonical prayer (*ṣalāt*) (29:45), insofar as it is the very substance of all possible prayer, and also its ultimate goal. One prays in order to be plunged into a state of concentrated awareness of the divine reality, and then to maintain this awareness permanently: 'In houses which God hath allowed to be elevated, and wherein His Name is invoked, He is glorified, morning and evening, by men whom neither trading nor bargaining distracts from the remembrance of God . . .' (24:36–37).

Therefore, one finds in this single verse, 1:5, a condensed summary of all the verses pertaining to worship, prayer, meditation and contemplation; and also all the verses pertaining to the virtues which prayer presupposes and which sincere prayer generates; and also all the verses describing the states of soul and the stations of realisation to which prayer and virtue lead—all of which are inherent to 'the straight path', to which the following verses refer. Before addressing these verses, though, we should note the intimate relationship between prayer and virtue that is stressed repeatedly throughout the verses of the Qur'ān. Some of these will be discussed below, suffice to say here that nearly every time the formal prayer, *al-ṣalāt*, is mentioned, it is conjoined with the notion of charity: the payment of *zakāt*. 'Those who establish *ṣalāt* and pay *zakāt*' is a constant refrain throughout the Revelation, such that the one can hardly be said to be complete without the other: prayer and charity go hand in hand, and are inseparable.

Returning to the state of soul of those who have reached the end of the path of spiritual perfection, it might be said that they no longer need to wait until the Day of Judgement to hear the words, 'O thou soul at peace', for it is as if these words are constantly ringing in their ears on earth. They are no longer seeking Paradise nor fearing Hell in their worship; they pray to God not for something as yet unattained, but on account of the plenitude of what they have already received: an already celestial degree of serenity, the fruit of the certainty of the beatitude which they have 'tasted' and not just thought about. This group are referred to by Imam 'Alī as those who are liberated, the 'free' (*al-aḥrār*):

> There is a group who worship God out of desire [for something not yet attained], and this is the worship of the merchants. And there is a group who worship God out of fear, and this is the worship of the slaves. And there is a group who worship God out of gratitude, and this is the worship of the free.[37]

This group of worshippers continue to pray, but do so on the basis of gratitude for what God has bestowed upon them by way of grace, wisdom, love and compassion. We thus return to the fundamental theme of the *Fātiḥa*, which is *Raḥma*. For this group are the ones who, having exerted themselves in the exercise of *tafaqquh* alongside their devotions, can be called true *fuqahā'*, bearing in mind the root meaning of *fiqh* as 'understanding', and recalling that the true *faqīh*, according to Imam 'Alī, is he who never makes people despair of the mercy of God. These *fuqahā'* have understood the reality of God as pure *Raḥma*, from which nothing can ultimately escape, by which all things were created, and to which all things return. As we shall see below, the Imam also describes these true *fuqahā'* as being those 'whose hearts are in the Gardens [of Paradise] while their bodies are at work [in this world]'. The body of the saint 'works' in this world according to the dispositions of a heart which is inspired not just by its vision of Paradise, but by its *presence* in Paradise, a spiritual presence which is permanent for the saints, who are distracted neither by 'trade nor merchandise' in this lower world from the 'remembrance of God'. Through the transformation of consciousness wrought by sincere, persistent and deep prayer, all believers are granted a taste of that paradisal reality in which the hearts of the Prophets, Imams and saints are permanently plunged.

Such is the importance of this intensity of prayer that the Prophet himself is instructed by God not to allow his attention to be deflected from those of his community most renowned for the intensity of their devotions: 'Restrain thyself along with those who cry unto their Lord at morn and evening, seeking His Countenance; and let not thine eyes overlook them, desiring the adornment of the life of the world' (18:28).

'*From Thee alone we seek help.*' Does this part of verse 5 imply that the seeking of help from the Prophets, the Imams and the saints is a form of *shirk*, an 'association' of other beings with the divinity, from whom, alone, all help is to be sought? Not at all. Again, there is an exoteric and an esoteric way of responding to this question. Exoterically, one need only refer to the words of the verse 4:64 to see that God not only permits but encourages the believers to seek the Prophet's prayers of forgiveness for them:

> . . . If only, when they had wronged themselves, they had come to thee, and pleaded for forgiveness from God, and had the Messenger pleaded for forgiveness on their behalf, they would indeed have found God to be clement and merciful (4:64).[38]

God responds mercifully not only to our own prayers of forgiveness, but also to those of the Prophet on our behalf; therefore, seeking the Prophet's 'help' is not an infringement of the principle of seeking 'help' from God alone, but is rather an aspect or specific application of this very principle. This is because God Himself has established various means by which He is to be approached, given His utter transcendence: 'seek unto Him a means of recourse (*wasīla*)' (5:35). The Qur'ān itself, together with all previous Revelations, the Prophet Muḥammad, together with all previous Prophets, the Imams and the saints of Islam and indeed of all religions—these are so many 'means' by which God can be approached, if the intention is indeed to resort to the means for the sake of the end, rather than be idolatrously fixated on the means as an end in itself. Then the prerogatives of *tawḥīd* are satisfied and one's seeking of help from these means is fully justified. The famous 'Throne verse' (*āyat al-kursī*) establishes the legitimacy of intercession—both as regards this world and the next:

> God—there is no God save Him, the Alive, the Eternal. Neither slumber nor sleep overtaketh Him. Unto Him belongeth whatsoever is in the heavens and whatsoever is in the earth. Who is he that intercedeth with Him save by His leave? He knoweth that which is in front of them and that which is behind them, while they encompass nothing of His knowledge save what He will. His Throne encompasseth the heavens and the earth, and He is never weary of preserving them. He is the Sublime, the Tremendous (2:255).

Esoterically, while the above reasoning will be confirmed, it will be reinforced by a perspective stemming from the vision of *tawḥīd* which is ontological (*wujūdī*) and not only theological (*ulūhī*). From this ontological point of view, as noted above, at verses 1–3 of the *Fātiḥa*, there is nothing in being but God; what appears as 'other than God' is a *maẓhar*, a locus for the manifestation of God and nothing else. When assistance is sought from the Prophets, the Imams and the saints, one is seeking assistance from them as so many manifestations of God, so many *maẓāhir*, or loci, of the *ẓuhūr* (manifestation) of *al-Ẓāhir*, the Outwardly Manifest. Therefore, the means as well as the end is divine: it is not a question of seeking human means for the sake of attaining a divine end, for one sees through the human form to the divine substance of the *maẓhar*. This is a radical mode of *tawḥīd*, a more penetrating application of the principle: *from Thee alone we seek help*. It also manifests metaphysical fidelity to the principle of divine ubiquity: 'Wherever ye turn, there is the Face of God' (2:115). It is this Face which is sought, both as regards the means and the end, when one seeks any kind of help from any kind of being: 'Every single good thing (*niʿma*) you have is [a grace] from God' (16:53).

The reference to *niʿma*—which can also be translated as 'blessing' or 'grace'—brings us back to the *Fātiḥa*, for the 'straight path' at verse

6 is described by reference to *alladhīna* ***anʿamta*** *ʿalayhim*, it is the path of 'those whom Thou hast blessed'. Esoterically speaking, those who have been most deeply blessed are those who see the divine Face 'im-pressed' upon every single thing. The *niʿma* is not only 'from' God in the sense of being an entity created by God; it is 'from' God in the sense of being a manifestation of God, and therefore it is divine in its essence, a ray of light which cannot be divorced from its source. This radical vision of ontological *tawḥīd*, this mode of assimilating all positive phenomena as manifestations of God, enables the heart of the true *muwaḥḥid*[39] to see that in seeking 'help' from anyone—and at any level—one is seeking help from nobody and nothing but God.

4. Guidance (verses 6–7)

Guide us upon the straight path;
The path of those whom Thou hast blessed; not the path of those who are subjected to anger, nor of those who go astray.

In these final two verses, the 'straight path' of divine guidance is contrasted with the path taken by those who sin and those who stray. All of the verses pertaining to guidance by God, and to its acceptance, refusal or neglect by human beings, are condensed into these two verses. The notion of guidance (*hidāya*) encompasses not just the legal injunctions and moral precepts found throughout the Qur'ān, but also all of the teachings and allusions found in the many narratives of the lives and missions of previous Prophets. Indeed, the 'straight path' which divine guidance opens up is far from restricted to Muslims alone. This is evident from all the verses in the text which refer so explicitly to other religions, and to the founders of those religions. It is made especially clear if we look at the category described in verse 7, 'those whom Thou hast blessed' (*alladhīna anʿamta ʿalayhim*). For this category is defined in more detail in another verse: ' . . . those whom God hath blessed (*alladhīna anʿama'Llāhu ʿalayhim*), among the Prophets, the saints, the martyrs and the righteous—and what excellent companions they are!' (4:69).

There is no limitation here, and it is in perfect accord with the thrust of the Qur'ānic message of religious plurality, that the 'straight path' be identified with the path followed by the Prophets and saints of all religions revealed by God. Indeed, one of the unique features of the Qur'ānic Revelation is precisely the degree to which the whole of humanity is addressed. This feature is manifest not just in several verses referring to all human beings, but also in the very fact that in the Qur'ān explicit mention is made of other religions, and that all human beings have received a revealed message from God: 'for every community (*umma*) there is a Messenger' (10:47). Even if the only religions explicitly mentioned in the Qur'ān are Judaism, Christianity, Zoroastrianism (and Sabianism), the other religions cannot be excluded from the 'straight path' of divine Revelation and guidance, for 'Truly, We sent Messengers before thee; among them are those about whom We have told thee, and those about whom We have not told thee' (40:78). Part of the Muslim's creed is to affirm belief in all previous Revelations: 'The Messenger believeth in that which hath been revealed to him from his Lord, and so do the believers. Each one believeth in God and His angels and His scriptures and His Messengers [the believers say]: We make no distinction between any of His Messengers . . .' (2:285).

Several other verses make clear the universal scope of the Qur'ān's teaching on the Revelations to mankind; the 'straight path' is one in essence, diversified in form, and it is the duty of the Muslim to affirm belief in this path to which all Prophets without exception have guided their communities. The following verse provides an important point of reference for this principle of universal guidance: 'Say [O Muslims]: We believe in God and that which is revealed unto us, and that which is revealed unto Abraham and Ishmael and Isaac and Jacob and the tribes, and that which was given unto Moses and Jesus, and the Prophets from their Lord. We make no distinction between any of them, and unto Him we have submitted' (3:84).

One may ask: why, then, are the religions so divergent in form if they are all guiding mankind to the 'straight path'? The Qur'ān answers: 'For each [community] among you We have appointed a Law and a Way. Had God willed, He could have made you one community. But that He might try you by that which He hath given you [He hath made you as you are]. So vie with one another in good works. Unto God ye will all return, and He will inform you of that about which ye differed' (5:48).

The unique essence of the 'straight path' is summed up in two essential qualities, faith and virtue. All spiritual teachings, ethical norms and legal precepts are intended to deepen these two qualities, which are expressed in the following verse as the fundamental pre-requisites or conditions for salvation:[40] 'Truly those who believe [in the Qur'ān] and the Jews and the Christians and the Sabeans—whosoever believeth in God and the Last Day, and performeth virtuous deeds—their reward is with their Lord; no fear or grief will befall them' (2:62; repeated almost verbatim at 5:69).

Turning now to the other two categories, 'those who are subjected to anger (*al-maghḍūbi ʿalayhim*)' and 'those who go astray (*al-ḍāllūn*)', we should note immediately that, contrary to so many mis-translations of this verse, God's 'anger' is not explicitly mentioned. This is of particular significance in light of the mercy that pervades the *Fātiḥa*: God is described as compassionate and merciful in two places, and the impact of this description is reinforced by the fact that the only direct act of which God is the agent, in the *Fātiḥa*, is the bestowal of blessing and grace: *anʿamta*, 'Thou hast blessed'. The implication here is that wrath and retribution are not essential, defining attributes of God, whereas mercy, compassion, love and radiant grace are. As noted above, for the mystics, God's 'anger' is only a word describing an accidental or contingent feature of 'the Real', *al-Ḥaqq*; it is a cipher for referring to the extrinsic consequence of a lack of receptivity on the part of man to the loving mercy which perpetually radiates from the pulsating heart of ultimate Reality. The anger in question, then, can just as easily be referred back to the souls themselves as to God, especially since, as already noted above, each soul will be given the 'book' of its deeds on the Day of Judgement and will be told: 'Read thy book. Thine own soul sufficeth this day unto thee as a reckoner' (17:13). The 'anger' in question can thus be interpreted as an anger directed against oneself, for one's own lack of receptivity to the *Raḥma* that was ever-emanating from the very substance of that Reality which is now seen in its true dimensions: 'Thou wast heedless of this', the sinner is told on the Day of Judgement, 'now We have removed from thee thy veil, and piercing is thy sight this day' (50:22). Seeing the ugliness of one's sins in the light of the absolute beauty of Reality cannot but result in anger and regret at one's misuse of the immense gifts of free will and intelligence: 'We warn you of a punishment at hand, a day when a man will look upon that which his own hands have sent before, and the disbeliever will cry: If only I were dust!' (78:40). Dust is a perfect symbol of the opposite of humanity: that which is utterly devoid of consciousness is by that very token devoid of responsibility. The sinner will long to be free from responsibility.

One might ask whether the sinners and the misguided can be truly regarded as responsible and free if God is described as *al-Muḍill*, 'He who leads astray' (on account of such verses as 39:37, 'He whom God sendeth astray, for him there is no guide'); and if the Qur'ān invites all to 'choose a way unto his Lord' and then immediately adds: 'Yet ye will not, unless God willeth' (76:29–30). One might answer this question in the following way. If one is 'rightly guided', then this is so by virtue of a possibility one has turned to positive account for oneself; if one is 'led astray', then one has only oneself to blame, for God's 'responsibility', even if He be described as *al-Muḍill*, is to be understood ontologically and not morally or anthropomorphically: we are morally responsible for what we do, God is 'ontologically' responsible for everything pertaining to Being. Part of the ontological responsibility of God entails the bringing into being of human responsibility and free will. If, by exercising this freedom badly, man commits sins, then he is led astray by his sin, not by God, for his sin acquires an existential momentum, which is referred to in the Qur'ān as an 'increase' in the disease of the heart: 'In their hearts is a disease, so God increased their disease' (2:10). Having chosen the slippery slope of sin, on the basis of their own free will, sinners will increase in sinfulness, due to the ever-accelerating momentum generated by each succeeding sin. God is the source of existence, and thus, the source of all the laws and rhythms and dynamics of existence at all levels—physical, moral, intellectual and spiritual; He is thus, in an ultimate sense 'responsible' for this particular law of existential momentum or 'sinful motion', according to which sins generate further sins. But God cannot be held responsible for man's initial decision to set out on this path of sin. That is man's responsibility, for which he will be held accountable. However, the 'disease' of the heart can be cured, instantly, at any moment, by the mercy which is a far more fundamental 'law' of existence, inscribed in the very heart of Being. All the sinner has to do is repent, and he will find that God will relent. As cited earlier: 'O My slaves, ye who have been extravagant to the detriment of your souls, despair not of the mercy of God. Truly God forgiveth all sins; He is indeed the Forgiving, the Merciful' (39:53).

This conception of the relationship between human responsibility and divine omnipotence as regards the nature of sin is finely articulated by Imam 'Alī in the following passage of the *Du'ā' Kumayl*:

> My God and my Protector! Thou put into effect through me a decree in which I followed the caprice of my own soul, and did not remain wary of the adornment fashioned by my enemy.[41] So he deluded me through my soul's caprice, and therein destiny favoured him. So in what was put into effect through me in that situation, I transgressed some of Thy statutes, and disobeyed some of Thy commands. But Thine is the argument against me, in all of that, and I have no argument in what Thy destiny put into effect through me therein . . .[42]

One should note here the combination between the 'ontological' power of God and the moral responsibility of man: there is an awareness that God is the ultimate source of the 'decree'—the possibility—according to which one is susceptible to sin; but this goes hand in hand with a deep sense of one's own moral responsibility for the sins committed. One does not blame God for one's sins: 'Thine is the argument (*al-ḥujja*) against me.' All that is left to do, upon realising one's culpability, is to implore the mercy of God: 'I find no place to flee from what occurred through me, nor any place of escape to which I turn in my affairs, other than Thine acceptance of my excuse, and Thy causing me to enter into the compass of Thy mercy'—the very mercy with which the entire supplication of Imam 'Alī begins: 'O God, I ask Thee by Thy mercy, *which embraceth all things*' (7:156).

A complementary principle to the above emerges from the Imam's description of Adam's being lured by 'the enemy' into committing the primal sin of disobedience in the Garden: 'But his enemy beguiled him, through envious desire for his immortal abode and his intimacy with the righteous. So Adam exchanged certainty for his doubt and resolution for his weakness.' The precise words of the Imam here are to be noted carefully: 'certainty' (*al-yaqīn*) is replaced by '*his* doubt' (*shakkihi*); 'resolution' (*al-'azīma*) is replaced by '*his* weakness' (*wahnihi*).[43] The Imam's use of the definite article for the positive elements (certainty and resolution), and the possessive pronoun, 'his', for the negative elements in Adam (doubt and weakness), can be read as a comment upon the verses of the Qur'ān cited above: 'Whatever good comes to thee is from God, and whatever evil comes to thee is from your own soul' (4:79); 'Every single good thing ye have is [a grace] from God' (16:53). All goodness, truth, beauty, virtue are rooted in the divine Reality, and thus cannot be said to be the 'possessions' of man, rather they 'belong' to God and are bestowed upon man; they are therefore qualities to which man has access, and in which he can participate, but cannot 'possess'. It is only their opposites that man comes to possess as his own, and this appropriation of negative properties—the disgrace or 'fall from grace'—takes place in the very measure of man's dereliction of the responsibilities entailed by being the recipient of these divine gifts.

These points are summed up in the following *ḥadīth qudsī*: 'O My servants, it is but your deeds that I take into account, and which I recompense; so let him who finds good praise God, and let him who finds other than that blame no one but himself.'[44]

Recommended *Sūras*

Sūrat al-Insān (76)

Man
(also referred to as: *al-Dahr*, 'Time')
In the Name of God, the Compassionate, the Merciful

[76:1]
Hath there come upon man any moment in which he was a thing unmentioned?
[76:2]
Truly, We created man from a drop of thickened fluid to test him; then We endowed him with hearing and vision.
[76:3]
Truly, We have shown him the way, be he grateful or ungrateful [or: disbelieving].
[76:4]
Truly, We have prepared for the ungrateful [disbelievers] manacles and carcans and a raging fire.
[76:5]
Truly, the righteous shall drink of a cup whereof the mixture is of Kāfūr,
[76:6]
A spring wherefrom the slaves of God drink, making it gush forth abundantly,
[76:7]
They keep their vow and fear a day whereof the evil is wide-spreading,
[76:8]
And feed with food the needy, the orphan and the prisoner, for love of Him,
[76:9]
[Saying]: 'We feed you, for the sake of God only. We seek no reward nor thanks from you;
[76:10]
Truly, we fear from our Lord a day of frowning and of fate'.

[76:11]
Therefore God hath warded off from them the evil of that day, and hath made them find brightness and joy;
[76:12]
And hath rewarded them for their patience: a Garden and silk attire;
[76:13]
Reclining therein upon couches, they will find there neither [scorching of the] sun nor bitter cold.
[76:14]
The shade thereof is close upon them and the clustered fruits thereof bow down.
[76:15]
Goblets of silver are brought round for them, and beakers of crystal
[76:16]
Crystals of silver, which they have proportioned in due measure.
[76:17]
There are they watered with a cup whereof the mixture is of Zanjabīl,
[76:18]
[From] a spring therein, named Salsabīl.
[76:19]
There wait on them immortal youths, whom, when thou seest, thou wouldst take for scattered pearls.
[76:20]
When thou seest, thou wilt see there bliss and high estate.
[76:21]
Their raiment will be fine green silk and gold embroidery. Bracelets of silver will they wear. Their
Lord will slake their thirst with a pure drink.
[76:22]
[And it will be said to them]: 'This indeed is a reward for you. Your endeavour is accepted'.
[76:23]
Indeed, We, even We, have revealed unto thee the Qur'ān, a gradual revelation;

[76:24]
So submit patiently to thy Lord's command, and obey not of them any guilty one or disbeliever.
[76:25]
And invoke the name of thy Lord at morn and evening.
[76:26]
And worship Him [a portion] of the night. And glorify Him through the livelong night.
[76:27]
Indeed, these love fleeting life, and put behind them [the remembrance of] a grievous day.
[76:28]
We, even We, created them, and strengthened their frame. And when We will, We can replace them, bringing others like them in their stead.
[76:29]
Truly, this is an Admonishment, that whosoever will may choose a way unto his Lord.
[76:30]
Yet ye will not, unless God willeth. Truly, God is Knowing, Wise.
[76:31]
He maketh whom He will to enter His mercy, and as for the wicked, He hath prepared a painful punishment for them.

* * *

It should be pointed out first of all that the 'occasion for revelation' (*sabab al-nuzūl*) of this chapter specifically concerned the Prophet's family, his 'Ahl al-Bayt'; the principle of selflessness central to the function of the imamate is also highlighted in the course of this chapter. According to both Shiʿi and Sunni sources, the family of Imam ʿAlī fasted on three consecutive days, going without food and breaking their fast only with water. One traditional account of the *sabab al-nuzūl* of this chapter is given as follows: Ḥasan and Ḥusayn had fallen ill, and the Prophet counselled Imam ʿAlī and Fāṭima to vow to God that they would fast for three consecutive days if their sons recovered. They made the vow (*nadhr*) and the boys recovered. The family (including their maid, Fiḍḍa) then fasted, and had only some barley-bread with which to break their fast at the end of the day. As they were about to break their fast, a beggar came and asked for food. The family gave away the bread they had prepared, and broke their fast with water, only. On the second day, it was an orphan who came in need, just as they were about to break their fast. Again, the holy family gave away whatever bread they had, and broke their fast with water. On the third day, a prisoner came and asked for food as they were about to break their fast; again, they gave away their barley-bread, and only had water with which to break their fast. It was after this event that the Prophet received the revelation of this Sūra.[1]

The actions and words of the holy family in relation to those whom they fed in this selfless manner contain significant lessons. First, the wretch, the orphan and the captive were given precedence over the children of the Imam and Hazrat Fāṭima, this compassion manifesting clearly their recognition of the equal humanity of those who were unrelated to them, but whose need they deemed greater than their own needs, or those of their own children. The act of compassion itself, arising out of the deepest spiritual motivation, demonstrates a key lesson for one's spiritual quest: it shows that the ethic of selfless generosity to others must be accompanied by an absence of any desire for personal reward, gratification, recognition, prestige, or even acknowledgement: one acts purely and simply 'for the sake of God'—one seeks neither 'reward nor gratitude' from those who receive one's help. This attitude combines compassion for one's fellow human beings with consciousness of one's ultimate aim: outward charitable action is predicated upon, and consolidates, inward spiritual aspiration. The synthesis between human compassion and spiritual consciousness transforms all acts of outward kindness into acts of inner purification, thereby adding a dimension of transformative spirituality to exemplary morality. As will be seen in our reflections on the *Sūrat al-Layl*, below, the 'most pious' (*al-atqā*) is described as one who 'giveth his wealth in order to purify himself; nobody possesseth any good thing which might constitute a reward for this person—for he seeketh only the Face of his Lord most High. And he, indeed, will be content' (92:18–21).

Contentment flows forth as the consequence of seeking only God's good pleasure, and not seeking any reward from those to whom one has been generous: the reward is given in abundance, and not just in the Hereafter, but also in this world: through the very contentment that arises in proportion to one's sincere intention to seek only God's good pleasure.[2] This intended orientation towards God is the dimension that adds spiritual depth and a divine quality to those acts of human compassion and selfless generosity towards one's fellow human beings.

One should also note the importance of the juxtaposition between gratitude and ingratitude at the beginning of the *Sūra*: 'Truly, We created man from a drop of thickened fluid to test him; then We make him hearing, knowing. Truly, We have shown him the way, whether he be grateful or ungrateful [or: disbelieving]'. Here, one places in brackets the word disbelieving as it is so heavily implied in the Arabic *kafūr*: fundamentally, the root *kafara* means 'to cover over'. Hence, the disbeliever (*kāfir*) is one who is ungrateful to his Creator, one who 'covers over' the truth of his origin, the source of his being, thereby indulging in the inescapable concomitant of disbelief: one takes oneself as one's 'god': 'Hast thou seen him who maketh his desire (*hawā*) his god?' (25:43; almost identical at 45:23). If one does not believe in God, one cannot but believe in one's ego as a kind of absolute, thus, as an idol, a substitute and rival to the true Absolute; the desires and whims of the ego then assume the character of quasi-absolute commands. Disbelieving in one's Creator thus engenders self-divinisation, the foreshadowing of which is complacency and self-satisfaction. 'Truly man becometh rebellious, insofar as he deemeth himself independent' (96:6–7).

The relationship between spiritual slavehood and ordinary piety is alluded to in the distinction between the 'slaves of God' (*'ibād Allāh*) and the 'righteous', at verses 5–6. The Ahl al-Bayt are implied as the exemplars of the 'slaves of God', for it is their actions that are described in the verses which follow, culminating in the feeding of others in preference to themselves. While 'the righteous' drink from a cup 'whereof the mixture is of Kāfūr', the slaves of God drink directly from the spring itself, 'making it gush forth abundantly' (76:5–6).

The 'slaves' drinking directly from the fountain are empty of themselves, and 'belong' entirely to the Lord, in contrast to the 'righteous' who retain, alongside their piety, a lingering sense of self-consciousness, by which they are partly 'possessed', and thus cannot belong wholly to God as do the 'slaves'. They can only drink from a cup flavoured by the fountain, not from the fountain itself. Only those who are utterly empty of their own egos, and who are thus filled by the presence of God, can drink directly from the fountain. But to be empty of one's ego is, from the relative point of view, a kind of death, from which the ordinary soul shrinks in fear: 'If ye claim that ye are the friends of God (*awliyā' Allāh*), singled out apart from (all) mankind, then long for death if ye are truthful' (62:6).

Esoterically interpreted, this challenge can be seen to underscore the relationship between spiritual extinction or *fanā'* and sanctity, or *walāya*. For it is only the *awliyā'* who can truly 'long' for this extinction which means death to egocentricity, in accordance with the Prophetic injunction: 'Die before you die'. One must die to one's egotism before physical death comes, and only the *awliyā'* can do this, or even want to do this, knowing that in this apparent 'death' resides true life, for the effaced slave becomes transparent to the Lord, and the very duality of slave-Lord is transcended, leaving only the divine oneness. This oneness is made apparent in the following remarkable saying by Imam 'Alī, which can be read as a commentary on the fountain of *Kāfūr*, and an intimation of what happens as a result of actually drinking from this fountain: 'Truly, God has a drink for His friends (*awliyā'ihi*). When they drink it, they are intoxicated (*sakarū*); and when they are intoxicated, they are enraptured (*ṭarabū*); and when they are enraptured, they are blessed (*ṭābū*); and when they are blessed they dissolve (*dhābū*); and when they dissolve, they are free (*khalaṣū*); and when they are free, they devote themselves purely (*akhlaṣū*); and when they devote themselves purely, they seek (*ṭalabū*); and when they seek, they find (*wajadū*); and when they find, they arrive (*waṣalū*); and when they arrive, they are at one (*ittaṣalū*); there is no difference between them and their Beloved.'[3]

This is how 'Abd al-Razzāq al-Kāshānī, author of one of the most important esoteric commentaries, describes the slaves who drink directly from the fountain of *Kāfūr*: 'The slaves are [themselves] the sources of this Fountain; there is no duality or otherness . . . were it otherwise, it would not be the Fountain of *Kāfūr*, because of the darkness of the veil of egotism (*anā'iyya*) and duality.'[4] Here, the aspect of union is further emphasised: the 'slaves' are, in their innermost substance, not other than the source or fountain from which they outwardly drink, and the paradisal fountain itself is a symbol of the divine Essence. The light of knowledge, guidance and virtue which emanates from these slaves is therefore nothing other than the light of God. Hence 'God is the Light of the Heavens and the earth', as the celebrated verse of light, tells us: 'light upon light'. This verse will be discussed further in relation to *Sūrat al-Takāthur*.

In this connection, it would be useful to note one of the most important of Imam 'Alī's esoteric sayings, which dramatically reveals the relationship between love and spiritual death, on the one hand, and between this spiritual death and the realisation of absolute *tawḥīd*—both relationships taking us to the very heart of the principle of *walāya*. The saying takes the form of a *ḥadīth qudsī*, a 'holy utterance' in which God is the speaker:

> Who seeketh Me, findeth Me,
> Who findeth Me, knoweth Me.
> Who knoweth Me, loveth Me,
> Who loveth Me, I love.
> Whom I love, I slay.
> Whom I slay, I must requite.
> Whom I must requite, Myself am the Requital.[5]

Also of great importance in this *Sūra* is the verse relating to the chief means by which one manifests gratitude: the remembrance of God. 'And invoke the name of thy Lord at morn and evening. And worship Him [a portion] of the night. And glorify Him through the livelong night.' We shall enter into further discussion of this theme in relation to the *Sūrat al-A'lā*, below.

Sūrat al-Aʿlā (87)

The Most High
In the Name of God, the Compassionate, the Merciful

[87:1]
Praise the name of thy Lord the Most High,
[87:2]
Who createth, then disposeth;
[87:3]
Who measureth, then guideth;
[87:4]
Who bringeth forth the pasturage,
[87:5]
Then turneth it to russet stubble.
[87:6]
We shall make thee read, so that thou shalt not forget,
[87:7]
Save that which God willeth. Truly, He knoweth the disclosed and that which still is hidden;
[87:8]
And We shall ease thy way unto the state of ease.
[87:9]
Therefore remind, for of use is the reminder.
[87:10]
He will heed who feareth,
[87:11]
But the most hapless will flout it,
[87:12]
He who will be flung to the great Fire
[87:13]
Wherein he will neither die nor live.
[87:14]
He is successful who groweth,
[87:15]
And remembereth the name of his Lord, so prayeth,

[87:16]
But ye prefer the life of the world,
[87:17]
Though the Hereafter is better and more lasting.
[87:18]
Verily, this is in the ancient Scriptures,
[87:19]
The Scriptures of Abraham and Moses.

* * *

This Sūra is a strong exhortation to engage deeply in *dhikr Allāh,* the remembrance of God, which implies the practice of the invocation of the Name of God, the single most important principle of all worship, as clearly stated in other verses of the Qurʾān, and in strongly attested sayings of the Prophet and the Imams. It is therefore one of the most essential pillars of the spiritual quest. The Qurʾān affirms that the very *raison d'être* of praying is to remember God: 'And establish the prayer for the sake of My remembrance (*aqim al-ṣalāt li-dhikrī*)' (20:14); the believers are told to 'remember God with much remembrance' (*dhikran kathīran*) (33:41); the remembrance of God is described as 'greater' than the formal prayer (*al-ṣalāt*): 'prayer keepeth one from indecency and evil, while the remembrance of God is greater (*wa la-dhikru'Llāhi akbar*)' (29:45). The Prophet referred to the *dhikr* as being the act bearing the richest reward from God, in numerous strongly attested sayings, all of which are summed up in Imam ʿAlī's description: 'the remembrance of God is the most excellent form of worship' (*afḍal al-ʿibāda*).[6]

In this *Sūra*, glorification of the 'Name of thy Lord' is given as a command in the first verse. This glorification (*tasbīḥ*) can take various forms—canonical prayers, personal supplications, Qurʾānic litanies, and so on—but the repetition of the divine Name as the most fundamental of these methodic practices can be deduced from the opening verse of this chapter, in conjunction with several verses, some of which we cited above. The command given to the Prophet in verse 9, 'Remind men, for of use is the reminder (*al-dhikrā*)', can be seen to allude to this principle. The stress on the remembrance of God is further reinforced by verses 14–17, where the 'successful' one is described as the one who 'remembereth the Name of his Lord (*dhakara'sma rabbihi*)', *and* prays—the *dhikr* is thus distinct from the *ṣalāt* in formal terms; in substantial terms, *ṣalāt* is a form of the *dhikr*, given that the latter is described as 'greater' than the former. The greater subsumes the lesser. The 'success' of the successful one is identified with true life in the Hereafter—which is 'better and more lasting'; whereas failure is implicitly identified with preference for 'the life of the world'. Here, the practice of the invocation is presented as the means par excellence whereby the Hereafter is given preference over the life of this world, whereby God is preferred over oneself. One whose orientation is to the *dhikr* rather than to the world is one who manifests and strengthens the orientation to the Hereafter. Duties and responsibilities in the world are not denied here; rather, these responsibilities are discharged all the more effectively insofar as they are accomplished with full awareness of God, rather than in a state of distraction from God. The Prophet is told, as partly cited earlier:

> O thou enwrapped in thy cloak,
> Stand in prayer all night, save a little—
> A half thereof, or lessen it a little
> Or add to it, and recite the Qur'ān in measured recitation.
> We shall charge thee with a weighty word.
> Indeed, impressions are more keen, and speech more penetrating, during the night.
> Truly by day thou hast many duties,
> So invoke the Name of thy Lord and devote thyself to Him with utter devotion (73:1–8).

It is to be noted in this passage that the many tasks of the Prophet to be performed during the day are not contradicted by, but rather, creatively juxtaposed with, the nocturnal practice of the remembrance, to which he should devote himself utterly. In other words, the spiritual practice deepens one's ability to perform one's worldly responsibilities rather than undermining it. The relationship between outer work and inner remembrance is one of reciprocal enhancement, not mutual exclusion. Imam ʿAlī makes this abundantly clear in his exhortation to Mālik al-Ashtar, in the course of his famous letter of instruction upon appointing him governor of Egypt. After detailing the complex duties and responsibilities incumbent upon him, he writes: 'Give unto God of your body [i.e., one's vital energy] in your nights and your days, and perform fully that by which you draw near to God, doing so perfectly, without becoming dull or deficient, taking your body to its limits (*bālighan min badanika mā balagha*).'[7] The reason for the necessity of this degree of exertion in the spiritual quest is summed up by the Imam in this analogy: 'He who prays without making an effort is like one who shoots arrows without a bow.'[8]

The complementarity between outward activity and inward contemplation is made clear by the Imam in his commentary on a Qur'ānic verse in which the remembrance of God is central. He cites the words 'men whom neither trade nor merchandise diverts from the remembrance of God' (24:37) at the beginning of one of his sermons (number 213 in the *Nahj al-balāgha*), and then proceeds to describe the 'men' in question in terms of the purifying power of the invocation and the mystery of spiritual enlightenment: 'Truly God has made the remembrance (*al-dhikr*) a polish for the hearts, by which they hear after suffering from deafness, and see after being blind . . . There have always been slaves of God . . . with whom He held intimate discourse through their thoughts and spoke with them through the essence of their intellects. They diffused illumination through the awakened light in their hearing and their seeing and their hearts, calling unto the remembrance of the days of God.'[9]

The commentary continues by describing the *ahl* or group who belong to the invocation, who have 'adopted it in place of the world', such that 'neither trade nor merchandise' distracts them from it. Their trade continues, but they are not distracted by it from the remembrance of God. This is because 'They spend the days of their life in it'—both in terms of methodic practice, at home and away from their work in the world, and in terms of being conscious of God, in principle, during their work in the world. 'It is as though they had left this world for the Hereafter, and they are there, witnessing what is beyond this world.' Here again the relationship between the invocation of the divine Name and the Hereafter is stressed: the invocation of God sows the seeds of a blessed Hereafter. Those who have given themselves up to a life of prayer and invocation are those who are already 'witnessing what is beyond this world'. But the Imam also shows that the invocation of God is not only about sowing the seeds of a wholesome life in the Hereafter, it is also about generating a more profound sense of justice in this life. For the people described as spending 'the days of their life' in the invocation are the very ones who 'instruct people about justice and themselves are steadfast therein'.

The following verse is important in this connection: 'Ask the folk of the remembrance (*ahl al-dhikr*) if ye know not' (16:43). Most Sunni commentators on this verse interpret the *ahl al-dhikr* as being those who were authorities within the pre-Qurʾānic Revelations among the People of the Book—which accords with the context of the words cited, as they are preceded by the words, 'And We sent not before thee other than men whom We had inspired'. However, Shiʿi commentators specify that the *ahl* in question are the Ahl al-Bayt. There is, however, no contradiction between the two interpretations: for the role and function of the Imams in Islam is prefigured by their counterparts in the previous religions, and indeed the Imams are deemed to be 'inheritors' of the various sciences and qualities associated with previous Prophets. In a strongly attested *ḥadīth*, we find Imam ʿAlī described in relation to previous Prophets: 'He who wishes to see Adam as regards his knowledge, Noah as regards his obedience, Abraham as regards his friendship [with God], Moses as regards his awe [of God], and Jesus as regards his purity, let him gaze upon ʿAlī b. Abī Ṭālib.'[10]

Those who belong to the *dhikr* are those who have given themselves up entirely to the *madhkūr*, the divine Reality invoked; and it is for this reason that, whatever their formal religion may be, they participate in the function of *walāya*, which is universal, and not restricted to any one particular religion to the exclusion of the others. Here one sees that the universal role of the Imam resonates both with the principle of the oneness of humanity and with the universal quest for enlightenment which defines the very purpose of religion and the goal of the human state.

Finally, returning to the message of verses 14–17 of the *Sūrat al-Aʿlā*, where success is identified with prayer, remembrance and spiritual growth, all of which stand as the antidote to the ego-driven preference for 'the life of the world', one should note the succinctness with which the true life Hereafter is described: it is, quite simply, 'better and more lasting' (*khayr wa abqā*). Not only is the life Hereafter eternal in contrast to life on earth which is ephemeral, but the quality of everything experienced in Paradise is 'better'—infinitely better, one might say. The mere thought of this eternal life is described in the Qur'ān as a 'purification': 'We purified them with a pure quality: remembrance of the Abode [of the Hereafter]' (38:46). All the descriptions of Paradise are thus to be read, pondered and deeply contemplated, such contemplation itself functioning as a mode of purifying oneself of excessive desire for this world, and thereby as spurs for one's quest for true 'success'. Imam 'Alī puts it thus: 'If you were to cast the eye of your heart towards what is described for you of the Garden, your soul would become averse to the marvels of this world—its passions, its pleasures and its embellished scenery. And your soul would be rapt in contemplation of the swaying trees whose roots lie hidden in dunes of musk on the banks of the rivers of the Garden, and the clusters of dazzling pearls hanging down from the branches of its trees . . .'[11]

Another key verse which should be borne in mind in relation to the spiritual quest for salvation is the verse: 'Whatever good ye send forth for your souls, ye will find it with God—better and greater in reward' (73:20). This is an expression of a universal principle: God will reward all acts of goodness in a manner that is incommensurably 'greater' than the acts themselves. Just as the Hereafter is 'better and more lasting', so one's acts of goodness in this world will bear fruit in goodness which is immeasurably better and everlasting. However, there is a continuity of essence which unites acts of goodness on earth and their celestial fruits in the Hereafter. This is expressed in the verse: 'Every time they [the souls in Paradise] are given to eat from its fruits, they say: This is what we were given before to eat. And they were given something similar thereto' (2:25).

The *Sūrat al-A'lā* concludes with an implicit reference to the unity of the spiritual message revealed by God to all of mankind, a theme which we discussed in relation to the *Fātiḥa*. This oneness of essence, which transcends all the formal differences between the religions, is alluded to by saying that the simple but profound truth expressed in verses 14–17 is found also in 'the former scrolls, the Books of Abraham and Moses'. Here the Revelations granted to Abraham and Moses are given as examples of the 'former scrolls', not in any exclusive manner, however, as there are Revelations and Prophets not mentioned in the Qur'ān: 'Truly, We sent Messengers before thee; among them are those about whom We have told thee, and those about whom We have not told thee' (40:78). The commentators record, in relation to this verse, that the Prophet was asked by Abū Dharr how many Prophets there were, how many Messengers there were, and how many revealed books there were. The Prophet replied, saying there were 124,000 Prophets, of whom 313 were Messengers (in addition to being Prophets), and that there were 104 revealed scriptures.[12] These numbers express the principle expressed elsewhere in the Qur'ān, that 'for every community (*umma*) there is a Messenger' (10:47). The human race is at one in respect of Revelation, therefore: every single community has received a divine message, and that message is in its essence one and the same, however diverse the different communities may be in terms of race, culture, language, etc. 'Naught is said unto thee [Muḥammad] but what was said unto the Messengers before thee' (41:43). Religion is therefore one, and is referred to as *al-dīn* ('the religion') in the following verse, which emphasises the inner unity of religion as such, subsisting beneath outwardly divergent forms assumed by religion: 'He hath ordained for you of the religion that which He commended unto Noah, and that which We reveal to thee [Muḥammad], and that which We commended unto Abraham and Moses and Jesus, saying: "Establish the religion, and be not divided therein" . . .' (42:13).

Here the unity of the human race is again stressed: be not divided in respect of the *essence* of religion, even if the *forms* of your religions may differ. That essence is described, again, with great simplicity: 'And We sent no Messenger before thee but We inspired him [saying]: "There is no God save Me, so worship Me"' (21:25). To the oneness of humanity corresponds the simplicity of the religious message, and the unicity and immutability of the spiritual quest, transcending time and space, race and religion.

Sūrat al-Shams (91)

The Sun

In the Name of God, the Compassionate, the Merciful

[91:1]
By the sun and its brightness
[91:2]
And the moon when it followeth it,
[91:3]
And the day when it revealeth it,
[91:4]
And the night when it enshroudeth it,
[91:5]
And the heaven and Him Who built it,
[91:6]
And the earth and Him Who spread it,
[91:7]
And a soul and Him Who perfected it
[91:8]
And inspired it [with consciousness of] what is wrong for it and right for it.
[91:9]
He is indeed successful who causeth it to grow,
[91:10]
And he is indeed a failure who stunteth it.
[91:11]
[The tribe of] Thamud denied in their rebellious pride,
[91:12]
When the basest of them broke forth
[91:13]
And the Messenger of God said: It is the she-camel of God, so let her drink!
[91:14]
But they denied him, and they hamstrung her, so God doomed them for their sin and destroyed their dwellings.

[91:5]
He feareth not the outcome.

* * *

Sun and moon, day and night, Heaven and earth: after mention of these complementary pairs, the soul is then described, and this in a manner which is of fundamental importance for the spiritual quest. The soul has been 'perfected' by the One in whom all perfection resides, infinitely and absolutely; the soul has been inspired with an inner disposition to discern between what is bad for it and what is good for it, the latter being described in terms of 'her piety' (*taqwāhā*). Success or deliverance is the fruit of the soul's proper nourishment, which is the responsibility of each and every individual. This inalienable personal responsibility for accomplishing one's spiritual obligations derives from the innate knowledge of good and evil, right and wrong, which is inscribed in the substance of each and every human soul, without exception.

The message of these verses as regards the principle of individual spiritual responsibility deriving from innate knowledge, is reinforced by the verse: 'And when thy Lord brought forth from the children of Adam, from their loins, their seed, and made them testify against their souls [saying], "Am I not your Lord?", they said, "Yes, verily, we testify." [This was] lest ye say on the Day of Resurrection, "Truly, of this we were unaware"' (7:172). This is known in the tradition as the 'Day of Alast', the day on which the question 'Am I not your Lord?' (*alastu bi-rabbikum*) is asked of each and every soul, at the very dawn of creation, when human consciousness was still in seed form, within the 'loins' of their archetypal forefathers. The message here is that nobody can use the pretext of ignorance to excuse their shortcomings on the Day of Judgement. Each soul not only knows the absolute reality of its Creator, it also knows, in the depths of its being, what it must do to be true and faithful to this source of its being. These verses, taken together, reveal the inescapable obligation attendant upon the human condition in its quest for spiritual progress. In doing so, they show what it means to be a human being: one is human to the extent that one strives to do justice to the spiritual possibilities inspired within—quite literally, 'breathed into'—the human soul by God: 'Then

He fashioned him [man] and breathed into him of His Spirit' (32:9). The spiritual quest is thus the quest to be fully human, according to the creative intention of God. These verses also implicitly stress the oneness of humanity, for it is clear that it is the human being as such who is being described. To be human means to strive to be spiritual; to strive to be true to the primordial and unalterable nature (*al-fiṭra*) of the human soul (to be discussed further, in relation to the *Sūrat al-Ikhlāṣ*, below).

Sūrat al-Layl (92)

The Night

In the Name of God, the Compassionate, the Merciful

[92:1]
By the night enshrouding,
[92:2]
And the day resplendent,
[92:3]
And Him Who hath created male and female,
[92:4]
Truly, your effort is dispersed [toward diverse ends].
[92:5]
As for him who giveth and is pious,
[92:6]
And affirmeth goodness,
[92:7]
Surely We will ease his way unto the state of ease.
[92:8]
But as for him who hoardeth and deemeth himself independent,
[92:9]
And disbelieveth in goodness;
[92:10]
Surely We will ease his way unto adversity.
[92:11]
His riches will not save him when he perisheth.
[92:12]
Truly, Ours it is [to give] the guidance.
[92:13]
And truly unto Us belong the latter portion and the former.
[92:14]
Therefore have I warned you of the flaming Fire,
[92:15]
Which only the most wretched must endure,

[92:16]
He who denieth and turneth away.
[92:17]
Far removed from it will be the most pious,
[92:18]
Who giveth his wealth in order to purify himself;
[92:19]
Nobody possesseth any good thing which might constitute a reward for this person—
[92:20]
For he seeketh only the Face of his Lord most High.
[92:21]
And he, indeed, will be content.

* * *

One of the key messages of this *Sūra* is the complementarity between generosity and piety, and how these two qualities must infuse the spiritual quest. In the verses which describe the 'pious', one should note that generosity is mentioned first of all: 'As for him who giveth and is pious, and affirmeth goodness, surely We will ease his way unto the state of ease.' This is contrasted with the miser, who not only hoards his wealth, he also deems himself independent of God. Such a person's denial of goodness is a logical consequence of his own miserliness. Conversely, the pious soul, who 'affirmeth goodness', does so in the very measure of his own generosity. This generosity is both a cause of the deepening of his piety and a consequence of that piety, and the state of soul to which piety and generosity lead is one of 'ease', in contrast to the adversity into which the miser falls. One should note here that the 'ease' in question is not simply to be seen as a future state, but one which characterises the condition of the generous, pious soul: ease is the defining feature of the soul of one whose piety and virtue are profound and operative, whereas adversity and hardship define the soul of the miser, who deems himself independent, and who suffers on account of the impossibility of ever reaching the desired state of independence. There is no security or ease for the miser who arrogantly denies his need of God, his need of others, his need to be generous.

The portrait of the pious soul is given a dimension of further spiritual depth and subtlety in the verses which complete the chapter. The 'most pious' (*al-atqā*) is described as giving his wealth generously to others, but this gift is not motivated by any desire for personal benefit, whether in the form of material reward, or the expression of thanks from the recipients of his gift, or in that more subtle form of egotism known as *ʿujb* in the spiritual tradition of Islam: a private and unspoken vanity taking the form of a sense of self-satisfaction—one silently congratulates oneself for being generous, taking pride in this act, instead of realising that God alone is the true sustainer—'the best of sustainers' (*khayr al-rāziqīn*) as the Qurʾān says in many places.

An outwardly generous person can easily be characterised inwardly by this self-satisfaction and by the desire to be praised for his generosity, and this not only undermines the spirit of his 'generosity', it fatally repels any authentic piety (*taqwā*), which is, essentially, the permanent consciousness of God. In the present context, it translates into a consciousness that, in being generous, one is merely giving out to others that which has been granted by God in the first place. Such is the description, given repeatedly in the Qurʾān, of the believers: they 'spend from the sustenance (*rizq*) which We have provided for them' (see 2:3 *et passim*). Therefore such souls do not fall into that subtle form of hypocrisy alluded to in the Qurʾān in the description of sinners who 'love to be praised for what they have not done' (3:188). God alone is *al-Karīm*, 'the Generous', and if a soul is generous, it is so as a grace from *al-Karīm*. Any attempt to claim credit for one's generosity is in effect a desire to be praised for what one has not actually done; and it is to enter into that state of adversity which characterises the miser who 'deemeth himself independent'—for the 'generous' person who is motivated by subtle vanity is implicitly desiring to expropriate a quality properly belonging only to God, and to glorify himself by means of that quality. Such a person implicitly 'deemeth himself independent', taking pride in his own quality instead of glorifying God.

The following verses describing the most pious help to further define the quality of soul of one who is generous, and whose generosity is motivated by authentic aspiration for God and not by any hidden motive for himself. He gives of his wealth not to glorify himself, but 'to purify himself'—to purify himself of all vices and deficiencies, including wrong intentions and motivations which might insinuate themselves, and thus poison, outwardly good acts. 'Nobody possesseth any good thing which might constitute a reward for this person.' There is no earthly reward, material or otherwise, that could motivate this person's generosity, because 'he seeketh only the Face of his Lord most High'. Seeking the Face (*wajh*) of God means to be motivated exclusively by the intention to give oneself to the essence of the Absolute, not to act or think except by reference to the Absolute. It is this absolute orientation to the Absolute which perforce relativises all other concerns. One is no longer motivated by desire for praise, nor fear of blame; one is no longer dependent upon what others may think or do in response to one's actions. This means that one's spiritual state is no longer determined by others, it is determined only by God, and for this reason, 'he, indeed, will be content'. One has access to imperturbable contentment in the measure that the object of one's actions is the immutable Absolute, the 'Face' of God, which is the source of all beauty, love and, thereby, liberating happiness. If the object of one's actions is anything other than the Absolute, then contentment will be forever out of reach: one's state of soul will be determined by the vagaries of relativity, whether external—in the form of the attitudes and actions of others—or internal—in the form of one's own unstable desires and fears.

This point is amplified by the attitude of the Ahl-Bayt towards the poor persons they fed, thus sacrificing their own food after fasting successively for three days, as noted above in relation to the *Sūrat al-Insān*: 'We feed you only for the sake of God [lit. 'for God's Face']; we desire neither reward from you, nor thanks' (76:9). This statement exemplifies the state of soul which is totally permeated and dominated by the consciousness of God, and which is fashioned by the selfless generosity which flows according to the profundity of that consciousness. It is to be noted that one of the most important verses revealing the *walāya* of Imam ʿAlī alludes to this same principle: 'Truly your guiding Master (*walī*) is only God, His Messenger, and the believers who perform the prayer, and give charity while bowing down' (5:55). In this verse, God is named as the 'Walī'—the Friend, the Guardian, the Master—all of which qualities are implied in the principle of *walāya*; but *walāya* also implies, secondarily, devotion to the source of authority, at whatever level, human or divine. For it is not just God who is named in this verse as the Walī of the believers, the Prophet is also referred to as Walī, along with the broad category of 'the believers'. But then this category is exemplified to perfection by one particular believer—Imam ʿAlī, who famously gave away his ring in charity while performing the *rukūʿ* (bowing) during the prayer.[13] This demonstrates clearly the continuity of the function of *walāya*, from the divine to the human; God's *walāya*, that quality of guardianship and love, patronage and guidance, defined essentially by infallible authority and unimpeachable holiness, is seen in this verse as extending into the human domain in this, one of the foundational verses of the Shiʿi doctrine of the imamate. What is to be noted here is the important role played by an act of outward charity in specifying the person invested with this sacred function of *walāya*. The outward act signals an inward disposition, one which wishes to give to others what one has been given oneself, both in the material and, pre-eminently, in the spiritual domain.

The relationship between outward material generosity and inward spiritual authority is further reinforced by the following verses, from the *Sūrat al-Baqara*: 'And whatever wealth you expend, God is indeed aware of it. Those who give their wealth by night and day, secretly and openly, their reward is with their Lord, no fear or grief will befall them' (2:274). It is the consensus among the commentators that the reference here is, again, to Imam ʿAlī; this consensus is based on the following highly corroborated report on the *sabab al-nuzūl*, the occasional cause of the Revelation. 'This verse was revealed about ʿAlī b. Abī Ṭālib who owned just four silver coins. He spent one coin at night, one coin during the day, one coin in secret and one in the open. The Messenger of God—may God bless him and give him peace—said to him: "What has motivated you to do this?" ʿAlī said: "My motivation is that God may grant me what He has promised me." The Messenger said: "Verily, you have it." In response to this, God revealed this verse.'[14]

In the measure that one identifies with these acts of compassion and charity, exemplified by the Imam, one comes closer to realising within oneself the spiritual principles or divine qualities upon which these acts are founded, and one comes closer to being effaced within those qualities, such that it is they, the divine qualities, that operate through the soul, rather than the soul claiming to possess the qualities: 'And thou didst not throw when thou threwest, but God it was who threw' (8:17). This verse also alludes to the principle of *walāya*, inasmuch as God is the 'hearing' by which the *walī* hears, the 'sight' by which he sees, the 'hand' by which he grasps, and the 'foot' by which he walks, as we noted in the *ḥadīth qudsī* cited in the introduction. All of the perceptions and the acts of the perfect saint are divine more than they are human, for God is the true agent of the one who has attained the degree of self-effacement before God, together with self-realisation in God, *al-fanāʾ fiʾLlāh* and *al-baqāʾ biʾLlāh.*

Knowledge that God is the true agent of all good or noble or successful actions is of the essence of 'slavehood' as will be seen shortly. Through emulation of the Imam, as regards both inward disposition and outward action, one not only enhances one's ethical comportment but also augments one's receptivity to the spirituality embodied by the Imam. One is thereby guided from outer example to inner principle, from the outer Imam to the inner Imam—the spirit of one's own intellect—whose potential is brought closer to fruition, and rendered more in harmony with the perfection manifested by the outer Imam.

Sūrat al-Ḍuḥā (93)

The Morning Brightness
In the Name of God, the Compassionate, the Merciful

[93:1]
By the morning brightness,
[93:2]
And by the night when it is still,
[93:3]
Thy Lord hath not forsaken thee nor doth He hate thee,
[93:4]
And verily the Hereafter will be better for thee than this life,
[93:5]
And verily thy Lord will give unto thee so that thou wilt be content.
[93:6]
Did He not find thee an orphan and protect thee?
[93:7]
Did He not find thee wandering and direct thee?
[93:8]
Did He not find thee destitute and enrich thee?
[93:9]
Therefore the orphan oppress not,
[93:10]
Therefore the beggar drive not away,
[93:11]
Therefore of the grace of thy Lord be thy discourse.

* * *

One of the basic messages of this *Sūra* as regards the spiritual quest is this: just as one has received protection and guidance and prosperity from God, one has a corresponding obligation to all those who are destitute, orphans, beggars, etc. Generosity to those in need will be manifested in the very measure that one is grateful for the blessings that one has received from God. One's awareness of the divine source of all of one's blessings is stressed in the final command: Of the grace of thy Lord be thy discourse. If one is aware that it is only through the grace of God that one has been guided, protected, and given sustenance, then it ought to follow that one has no right to be miserly with those same blessings, but, on the contrary, one must manifest one's gratitude to God through generosity to others. As cited earlier: 'Every single good thing you have is [a grace] from God' (16:53); 'Whatever good comes to you is from God, and whatever evil comes to you is from your own soul' (4:79). Since one possesses nothing on one's own account, everything good being a grace from God, it follows that the graces granted to one must be shared with others, and not selfishly kept to oneself out of greed.

Generosity to others is thus a function of one's detachment from one's own selfishness, and this detachment is made all the more natural and effortless to the extent that one is aware that God is the true 'owner' of all good things, material and spiritual; one must be aware that these goods are on loan to us, as a test, as these verses from the *Sūrat al-Fajr* show: 'As for man, when his Lord trieth him by honouring him and is gracious to him, he saith: My Lord honoureth me!' (89:15). The graces granted to man by his Lord are there to test him, not in order for him simply to glorify himself. The verses following this one in the *Sūrat al-Fajr* make clear the consequences of selfishness and hard-heartedness, which stem from a failure to recognise that God is the true possessor of all wealth:

> But when He trieth him by straitening his means of life, he saith:
> My Lord despiseth me!
> Nay, but ye honour not the orphan,
> And urge not the feeding of the poor,
> And ye devour heritages with devouring greed,
> And love wealth with abounding love (89:16–20).

Sūrat al-Inshirāḥ (94)

The Expansion
In the Name of God, the Compassionate, the Merciful

[94:1]
Have We not expanded thy breast for thee,
[94:2]
And lifted the burden from thee,
[94:3]
That which weighed heavily upon thee,
[94:4]
And exalted thy renown for thee?
[94:5]
But indeed, after hardship cometh ease,
[94:6]
Indeed, after hardship cometh ease.
[94:7]
So when thou art relieved, still strive,
[94:8]
And long for thy Lord with ardent desire.

* * *

The assurance is given in this *Sūra*, as in the previous one, that 'after hardship cometh ease'. The 'expansion' of the breast here is a symbol for the state of ease which will always follow a state of hardship, in the very measure that one's spiritual aspiration be resolute. This means that in the face of trials and tribulations one must always maintain patience, in the absolute certitude that divine grace will come, sooner or later, and that all difficulties in life are tests of our faith. The following passage on those who manifest the cardinal virtue of patience helps one to appreciate the spiritual importance of maintaining trust that 'after hardship cometh ease':

> O ye who believe, seek help in patience and prayer. Indeed, God is with the patient. And call not those who are slain in the way of God dead. Nay, they are alive, but ye perceive not. And We shall try you with something of fear and hunger and loss of property and life and fruits; but give glad tidings to the patient—those who, when struck by affliction say: 'Truly, we belong to God and truly unto Him we are ever-returning.' These are the ones upon whom there are blessings from their Lord, and mercy; and these are the ones who are rightly guided (2:153–157).

One is called upon not just to be patient in the face of trials, but also to open oneself up to the 'blessings' and the 'mercy' that descend from God in the very midst of the trial, if one responds to the trials with strong faith, manifested in the saying 'truly we belong to God and truly unto Him we are ever-returning' (*innā li'Llāhi wa innā ilayhi rāji'ūn*). One of the spiritual messages of the *Sūrat al-Inshirāḥ* is complementary to this principle of patience in the face of trials: for one is told that one must 'strive' and persevere in one's spiritual endeavour, even (or especially) when one has been granted relief from hardship. In other words, when one is no longer oppressed by any 'burden' or difficulty, and one finds oneself in a state of ease, one must continue to be fervent in one's spiritual quest, and not fall into complacency or laziness. The final words of this *Sūra* are to be noted: 'long for thy Lord with ardent desire' (*wa ilā rabbika fa'rghab*). The word *raghba* means fervent, loving, ardent desire. It is this quality which should infuse our spiritual quest at all times and, in particular, when we find ourselves in a state of ease or in a privileged situation. This is a spiritual application of the traditional ethical precept: *noblesse oblige* (i.e., when one has received the privileges of nobility, one's obligation to society, and in particular those less fortunate than oneself, is correspondingly deepened).

Sūrat al-Tīn (95)

The Fig
In the Name of God, the Compassionate, the Merciful

[95:1]
By the fig and the olive,
[95:2]
By Mount Sinai,
[95:3]
And by this land made safe;
[95:4]
Surely We created man in the finest stature
[95:5]
Then we reduced him to the lowest of the low,
[95:6]
Save those who believe and do good works, and theirs is a reward unfailing.
[95:7]
So who henceforth will give the lie to thee about religion?
[95:8]
Is not God the most conclusive of all judges?

* * *

The universality of Revelation is implicitly referred to in the beginning of this *Sūra*, since the fig and the olive are interpreted as symbols for a mountain in Syria, frequented by various Prophets, and Abraham in particular, and the mount of olives in Jerusalem, associated with Jesus; mount Sinai refers to the Mosaic Revelation and 'this land made secure', to Mecca. The unity of mankind is thus implied in this affirmation of the plurality of forms of Revelation through time and space. The relationship between the universality proper to unity and the particularity proper to multiplicity is also implied in the very symbolism of the fig and the olive. Kāshānī, for example, refers to the spiritual sciences of 'universals' contained within the undifferentiated unity of the fig—all of its seeds, symbolising the universal possibilities contained within the one 'body' of the fruit. The fig is thus compared to the heart, which perceives universals. The olive, on the other hand, with its single stone, symbolises the particularities of knowledge and being. It is compared to the soul, which perceives particulars.[15]

The reference to man being created in the finest stature also relates to the unity of the human race, reinforcing the oneness of the *fiṭra* of the human being. This finest stature, the *fiṭra*, pertains to each and every human being, whatever be the form of the beliefs they come to adopt through extrinsic religious conditioning, or through the negation of religion. To be 'human' means to be defined by the *fiṭra*, and to have access to all the potential comprised within this divinely ordained predisposition to spiritual truth and moral perfection. All human beings therefore remain one and, ultimately, indivisible according to this deepest level of their primordial and immutable nature. What should be stressed here is that this primordial nature is described both in terms of 'God's creation', which cannot be changed, and with the 'right religion', which cannot be superceded: 'There is no altering God's creation. That is the right religion (*al-dīn al-qayyim*), but most people know not' (30:30).

The fact that 'there is no altering God's creation' means that this primordial nature can be obscured but never abolished: all human beings are as one insofar as their innermost nature is this *fiṭra*, which, in turn, is patterned according to the nature of God Himself, *al-Fāṭir*, 'The Originator'. Just as God is one in essence, so too is the human race one in essence. 'Truly God created man in His own form (*inna'Llāha khalaqa'l-insān fī ṣūratihi*)', according to a saying of the Prophet, echoing the biblical verse: 'God made man in His own image' (Genesis, 1:27). This oneness of the human race is affirmed in several other verses, among the most important of which is this one: 'Your creation and your resurrection [O people] are but as [the creation and resurrection of] a single soul' (31:28).

The verse 'then We reduced him to the lowest of the low' can be interpreted as a warning: those who do not strive to be true to the 'finest stature', to the spiritual potential inherent in their own human nature, will find that they are reduced to a state which is beneath that of the animals. For a human being untrue to the human vocation is lower than the animals, who can do nothing but follow the dictates of their God-given nature. Those human beings who 'have hearts with which they understand not, and eyes with which they see not, and ears with which they hear not' are described as being 'like cattle—nay but they are worse! They are the neglectful' (7:179). The 'neglectful' or 'heedless', *al-ghāfilūn*, are the very opposite of those who remember, *al-dhākirūn*. Those who 'remember God' by means of their God-given faculties—hearts, eyes and ears representing the whole range of human consciousness in this verse, 7:179—are those who are true to their God-given nature. Those who, on the contrary, neglect their spiritual obligations will find not only that they become ever more susceptible to sin, but also blind to the reality of God: 'their hearts have become rusted by that which they have done' (83:14). This rusted heart is also referred to in the Qur'ān as a 'disease', the disease of hypocrisy: 'And among mankind there are those who say: "We believe in God and the Last Day", while they believe not. They think they are deceiving God, but they deceive none but themselves; and they perceive not. In their hearts is a disease, and God increaseth their disease' (2:8–10).

As noted in our discussion of the last verses of the *Fātiḥa*, one cannot in any way blame God for one's own misdeeds, or for reducing man 'to the lowest of the low', as it is put in this chapter: man reduces himself to this abject state by his own neglect and heedlessness, bringing upon himself the disease of hypocrisy and sinfulness. The fact that God is described as increasing this disease, as noted earlier, can be understood ontologically and not volitively, morally or anthropomorphically: in other words, God does not wilfully intensify the disease, but once it is rooted in the heart, it intensifies by virtue of the propulsive force proper to Being. Since there is no force or power in Being but God, one can say, figuratively speaking, that God 'increases' the disease of the heart of the sinner. However, returning to the *Sūrat al-Tīn*, the very next verse emphasises the ever-present possibility of being cured of this spiritual disease: 'Except those who believe and perform virtuous deeds.' It is virtue allied to faith that saves one from being reduced to the 'lowest of the low'. Imam 'Alī reinforces the contrast between the neglectful soul, the *ghāfil* who, by forgetting God, allows his heart to become diseased, and the recollected soul, the *dhākir* who, by remembering God, is cured of this disease. He addresses God as follows in his famous *Du'ā' Kumayl*: 'O Thou whose Name is a remedy and whose invocation is the cure (*yā man ismuhu dawā' wa dhikruhu shifā'*).'[16]

Sūrat al-Qadr (97)

Power
In the Name of God, the Compassionate, the Merciful

[97:1]
Truly, We revealed it on the Night of Power.
[97:2]
And what will convey unto thee what the Night of Power is!
[97:3]
The Night of Power is better than a thousand months.
[97:4]
The angels and the Spirit descend therein, by the permission of their Lord, with all decrees:
[97:5]
Peace, therein, until the rising of the dawn.

* * *

This is one of the most often recited chapters in the daily prayers of the Shiʿis, second only to the *Sūrat al-Ikhlāṣ*, which we address below. Outwardly, this chapter describes the revelation to the Prophet of the Qurʾān, in its entirety, in synthesised form, on one of the odd nights during the last ten nights of Ramadan; inwardly, or esoterically, the 'Night of Power' is interpreted as an allusion to the very soul of the Prophet. Exoterically, the particular verses of the Qurʾān are deemed to have descended 'upon' the heart of the Prophet (26:192–194); but esoterically the essence of the Qurʾān is deemed to have descended *into* the heart of the Prophet. Kāshānī, for example, tells us that the Night of Power is 'the Muḥammadan constitution in a veiled state'—that state in which, alone, he can receive Revelation, after having had 'essential vision', that is, of the Essence beyond forms, and thus, beyond Revelation.[17] What this kind of interpretation alludes to is the spiritual power inherent in the absolute receptivity of the state of the Prophet's soul. This receptivity can also be considered as total emptiness, and thus as *faqr*; and, at the highest level, as *fanāʾ*, a state of total extinction from oneself. Applied analogically to the spiritual quest, it can be said that every soul must make itself into a kind of 'Laylat al-Qadr', by emptying itself of egotism and worldliness, in order to be 'full' of receptivity to the divine; one aims to become a vessel made empty for the influx of divine grace.

As noted in our discussion of the *Fātiḥa*, one of the Prophet's epithets is *al-Nabī al-ummī*, 'the unlettered Prophet'. This clearly signifies the *faqr* and, at the deepest level, the *fanā'*, which characterise the Prophetic degree of receptivity to divine revelation. This 'emptiness' on the plane of the soul translates not only into a perfect fidelity in transmitting the divine message; it also implies an unsurpassable perfection of character. For emptiness of the qualities of the ego implies fullness of the qualities of God. It is for this reason that the heart of the Prophet is compared in Islamic spirituality to a spotless mirror; there is no 'spot' or trace of individualism or egocentricity which might prevent the qualities of God from being reflected by the heart of the Prophet. Being a perfect saint, *walī Allāh*, the Prophet does not obstruct the flow of the divine through his being. As we saw earlier, the perfect *walī* is he who is loved by God to the point where the divine reality becomes 'his hearing by which he hears, his sight by which he sees, his hand by which he grasps, and his foot by which he walks'. To follow and emulate the Prophet thus implies imbibing the very qualities of God by which the Prophet is both penetrated and effaced: 'Truly those who pledge allegiance to thee [O Prophet] are only pledging allegiance to God. The Hand of God is over their hands' (48:10).

This manifestation of divine reality through the spiritual 'constitution' of the Prophet—through him as the *Laylat al-Qadr*—by no means entails a reduction of the divine to the human. It does not, in other words, imply *shirk*. Rather, it implies the most radical display of *tawḥīd*. For the Prophet's soul, being utterly effaced before God, allows the oneness of God to display its various modes of perfection, unimpeded by any individualistic veils; those perfections of unity, or the divine qualities, which *can be* manifested *will be* manifested—and to perfection—through the effaced soul of the Prophet. The human manifestation of virtue becomes but an appearance; the reality of this manifestation is purely divine: 'And thou didst not throw when thou threwest, but God it was who threw' (8:17), God tells the Prophet.

In one of the most popular devotional poems in praise of the Prophet in the tradition of Islamic piety, the *Burda* of al-Buṣīrī, we read the following: 'Truly, the bounty (*faḍl*) of the Messenger of God has no limit, such that a speaker might be able to verbally articulate it.'[18] One might retort that it is only the divine bounty that has no limit. No doubt al-Buṣīrī would reply that every aspect of the Prophetic bounty is ultimately nothing other than that of God: 'Every single good thing ye have is [a grace] from God' (16:53). The bounty—and indeed every quality—manifested by the Prophet is not egoistically claimed or misappropriated by him. So every attribute manifested by Him can only be divine, unsullied by the impurities of relativity: 'Truly God only wishes to remove from you all impurity, O Ahl al-Bayt, and to purify you with a complete purification' (33:33). The Prophet's virtues, then, are not his own; they must be seen as the reflections of qualities which are ultimately, or metaphysically, God's own Names and Attributes. These virtues are human and created in form, but divine and uncreated in essence. When, therefore, he is described as *ra'ūf*, 'kind', and *rahīm*, 'merciful' (9:128), one cannot but see these traits, according to the metaphysical logic of *tawḥid*, and in the light of the effacement of the Prophet, as being reflections of the divine qualities, *al-Ra'ūf*, and *al-Raḥīm*. Herein lies one of the meanings of the 'tremendous character' (*khuluq 'aẓim*) ascribed to the Prophet (4:68); one should note that *al-'Aẓim*, also, is one of the Names of God.

The spotless mirror, the Prophet's heart as the *Laylat al-Qadr*, not only reflects faithfully the light of the Qur'ān revealed to him; it also reflects the very Face of God, that Face which the Qur'ān tells is visible, in principle, wherever we may turn (2:115). However, in practice, this Face is veiled by all but the greatest Prophets and saints. They alone have achieved that degree of effacement required for the removal of the veil of egocentricity, their souls have become translucent, thereby permitting the theophany of the Face of God to transpierce, and radiate through, their empirical form. This perspective on the Prophet as the perfect mirror for divine self-revelation—that is, God revealing *Himself* through *tajallī*[19] and not only revealing *His message* through *tanzīl*—is summed up in the following lines of 'Abd al-Raḥmān Jāmī (d. 1492), who addresses the Prophet: 'God made you the mirror of the Essence. A looking-glass for the unique Essence.'[20]

Metaphysically, then, all praise of the Prophet is praise of the image of the Face of the Essence reflected in the pure mirror of his heart. It is thus praise of God and hence remembrance of God,[21] if one has the appropriate spiritual vision; that is, if one can perform the *ta'wīl* (literally:

take back to the beginning) required to follow the reflection back to its source. The reflected image of the Face then rejoins the Face as such, which is independent of and infinitely transcends the mirror reflecting it. Needless to say, the Prophet as the human embodiment of perfection is also being praised—the very name, *Muḥammad*, means 'the praised'; but from the point of view of *tawḥīd* as 'integration', the praise of the Prophet is integrated within praise of God. Through this integration, praise of the Prophet acquires more, rather than less significance.

Truly, God and His angels bless the Prophet; O ye who believe, bless him and greet him with peace (33:56). Upon the revelation of this verse, the Prophet was asked how one was to perform this blessing, and he replied with this formula: 'O God, bless Muḥammad and the descendants of Muḥammad, as Thou hast blessed Abraham and the descendants of Abraham. Truly, thou art the Praised, the Glorious . . .' Such is the importance of this blessing that the prayers are incomplete without it—and this applies both to Sunni and Shiʿi schools of law. In the lines of a poem written by the founder of one of the four schools of Sunni law, al-Shāfiʿī:

> Loving you, O family of the household of the Prophet of God,
> Is an obligation (*farḍ*) from God in the Qurʾān which He revealed;
> Sufficient to show the grandeur of your dignity
> Is that one who blesses you not—no prayer has he.[22]

The Prophet told his followers that whoever blesses him once receives a ten-fold blessing in return. One can understand this ten-fold blessing in a variety of ways, some more obvious than others. Certainly, one of the ways in which this blessing manifests is that one's loving emulation of the Prophet serves to displace egotism, so that one comes closer to that perfect receptivity symbolised by the *Laylat al-Qadr*. To emulate the Prophet is to emulate a human model of perfection that is at once 'supreme' and yet accessible to each and every human being. While some may regard this emulation as leading to a kind of conformism, those within the tradition of Islamic piety understand that it does nothing of the kind; rather, it sharpens the very contours of one's unique, God-given personality by harmonising the configuration of personal qualities with one's primordial human nature, the *fiṭra*, so perfectly realised by the Prophet.[23] It is in this mystical sense that one can understand the verse which tells us that the Messenger is 'from yourselves': 'Truly there hath come unto you a Prophet from yourselves' (9:128). Though conventionally understood as meaning 'a human being, like yourselves', it can also be understood in terms of a more profound principle of spiritual identity. This principle is well articulated by Rūmī in his explanation of this verse:

> In the composition of man all sciences were originally commingled so that his spirit might show forth all hidden things, as limpid water shows forth all that is under it . . . and all that is above it, reflected in the substance of water. Such is its nature, without treatment or training. But when it was mingled with earth or other colours, that property and that knowledge was parted from it and forgotten by it. Then God Most High sent forth Prophets and saints, like a great, limpid water such as delivers out of darkness and accidental colouration every mean and dark water that enters into it. Then it remembers; when the soul of man sees itself unsullied, it knows for sure that so it was in the beginning, pure, and it knows that those shadows and colours were mere accidents. Remembering its state before those accidents supervened, it says, 'This is that sustenance which we were provided with before.'[24] The Prophets and the saints therefore remind him of his former state; they do not implant anything new in his substance. Now every dark water that recognises that great water, saying, 'I come from this and I belong to this,' mingles with that water . . . It was on this account that God declared: 'Truly there hath come unto you a Prophet from yourselves.'[25]

If the spiritual quest be defined as emulation of the Prophetic perfection, then the verses in the Qur'ān which give us a description of the soul of the Prophet are of immense operative and indeed transformative value. The Prophet is referred to as a 'most beautiful example' (*uswa ḥasana*; 33:21), and it is the beauty of his example that stands out above all else in the Qur'ānic descriptions of his character. The qualities described in the following verses can be seen as so many expressions of the beauty of soul which flows from one who is devoid of egotism, who has thereby become capable of receiving revelation—whose heart has thus become a veritable 'Night of Power':[26]

- There hath come to you a Messenger from yourselves, grievous for him is what distresses you, he is full of deep concern for you, kind and compassionate to the believers (9:129).

- We only sent thee as a mercy (*Raḥma*) to all of creation (21:107).
- It was by the mercy of God that thou wast gentle with them; for if thou hadst been harsh and hard-hearted they would have scattered from you. So pardon them and ask forgiveness for them and consult them in affairs (3:159).

When, therefore, the Prophet's character is referred to as 'tremendous' (*ʿaẓīm*), this is to be understood first and foremost in terms of the sanctity, magnanimity and wisdom from which loving compassion emanates as the most fundamental quality on the human plane. We see here another aspect of Imam ʿAlī's saying that the whole of the Qurʾān is contained in the *Fātiḥa*, which itself is contained in the phrase *bismi'Llāh al-Raḥmān al-Raḥīm*:[27] the Prophet's soul is itself one with the Qurʾān, the *Fātiḥa* and the *basmala*. This quality of *raḥma* permeates the whole of the Qurʾān and the whole of the soul of the Prophet as 'container' of the Qurʾān, that is, as *Laylat al-Qadr*: it is this quality above all others that one must 'follow' when one follows the Prophet: 'If ye love God,' the Prophet is told to say to the believers, 'follow me; God will love you' (3:31).

Finally, it would be well to consider the following famous saying of the Prophet: 'I was sent *only* for the sake of perfecting the most noble virtues' (emphasis added). These noble virtues, *makārim al-akhlāq*, attain their perfection in the soul only through a complete orientation to the divine source of all human virtues. In other words, they attain their plenitude only on the basis of the emptiness of the human soul, symbolised by the Prophetic perfection as the 'Night of Power'. Then the noble virtues of the soul contribute to the spiritual quest; any appropriation of these virtues to oneself, by contrast, poisons one's spiritual aspiration. It is for this reason that Imam ʿAlī says: 'The sin that grieves you is better, in the sight of God, than the virtue that makes you proud.'[28] If virtue is allied to spiritual poverty, then it becomes a mode of prayer; for it then becomes a faithful reflection of the divine quality of which it is a prolongation. The Prophet, as the beautiful example, the 'Night of Power', helps his followers to attain this degree of spiritually transformative virtue through being the spotless mirror in which the transcendent and thus unknowable Essence reveals something of its infinite qualities.

Sūrat al-ʿĀdiyāt (100)

The Coursers
In the Name of God, the Compassionate, the Merciful

[100:1]
By the snorting coursers,
[100:2]
Striking sparks of fire
[100:3]
And scouring to the raid at dawn,
[100:4]
Then, therewith, with their trail of dust,
[100:5]
Cleaving, as one, the centre (of the foe),
[100:6]
Truly man is an ingrate unto his Lord
[100:7]
And indeed he is a witness unto that;
[100:8]
And truly in the love of good he is violent.
[100:9]
Knoweth he not that, when the contents of the graves are poured forth
[100:10]
And the secrets of the breasts are made known,
[100:11]
On that day will their Lord be perfectly informed concerning them.

* * *

A key verse here concerning the spiritual quest is this: 'And truly in the love of good he is violent' (*innahu li-ḥubbi'l-khayri la-shadīd*). Most commentators interpret this to mean that the disbeliever lets himself get carried away with his intense attachment to wealth—one of the 'good' things in life. While this is evident, there is a deeper meaning which can be construed as a warning also to the believer: for the verse might also be seen as alluding to a more subtle form of materialism which afflicts the believer, despite his belief in God and the Hereafter. Instead of balancing one's appreciation of the goods of this world with the goods of the Hereafter, one's desire for the goods of this world attains such intensity (*shidda*) that the goods of the Hereafter are in fact marginalised: one's *de facto* aims, orientations, desires, are focused on things of this world, to the virtual exclusion of spiritual values and aspirations, even if such values and aspirations be paid lip-service. Desire for terrestrial goods eclipses the aspiration for celestial felicity.

Even if the things of the world are 'good' in themselves, they acquire the character of temptations and distractions if they obscure the much greater goods of the Hereafter—those goods which are prefigured in the world by heartfelt faith, profound virtue, sincere worship and spiritual knowledge. One of the most important supplications taught by the Qur'ān in this connection is the following: 'Our Lord, grant us the good things of this world, and the good things of the Hereafter, and protect us from the punishment of the Fire' (2:201). This integral and balanced supplication is given after mention is made of the incorrect, unbalanced supplication made by those who may believe in God and the Hereafter in principle, but this ostensible belief does not prevent them from being materialistic in practice: 'Our Lord, grant us [the good things] in this world.' For them, the Qur'ān says, 'there is no share in the Hereafter' (2:200). The spiritual quest does not require one to ignore the goods of the world; but it does require that they be desired in a manner proportionate to their relative value. The only thing that should be desired in an absolute manner is the Absolute. The verse in question, and the whole *Sūra,* is a reminder of the need always to maintain a correct sense of spiritual proportions.

Imam 'Alī imparts a radical lesson about a spiritual sense of proportions when he speaks in one of his sermons about his 'brother in God' (*akh fi'Llāh*)—commentators opine that he is speaking of Abū Dharr al-Ghifārī: 'What made him great in my eyes was the smallness of the world in his (*yu'aẓẓimuhu fī 'aynī ṣighar al-dunyā fī 'aynihi*).'[29] This sums up succinctly the attitude of *zuhd*, which we might translate, albeit somewhat wordily, 'deeming the world of little worth';[30] an attitude for which Imam 'Alī was so renowned, and which he expects to find in the souls of all those who maintain that they are 'believers'. This applies even more to those who claim to have knowledge of this world: 'He who knows the world withholds himself from it (*man 'arafa'l-dunyā tazahhad*).'[31]

However, returning to the principle of spiritual proportions, one must note that Imam 'Alī also waxes lyrical about the beauty and grandeur of this world, insofar as they are grasped as 'signs' of God, and not insofar as they are doomed to perish, nor insofar as they are isolated from their Creator and thus *de facto* worshipped as idols. The beauties of the natural world—such as the spectacular kaleidoscope unfolded by the peacock[32]—are described with majestic eloquence by the Imam in many passages of the *Nahj al-balāgha*. These passages can be seen as complementary to the stern renunciation of the world for which the Imam was renowned, and they can also be seen as responses to the repeated invitation of the Qur'ān to meditate on the 'signs' of God furnished by the splendours of the natural world. 'And there is nothing that does not hymn His glory with praise' (17:44). This means that everything in the world, all the creatures in existence, cannot help proclaiming, by means of their very existence, the marvellous creativity of their Creator. The Qur'ān is replete with concrete images helping us to glimpse the mystery of this universal and inescapable praise offered up to God by all creatures. For example as cited earlier: '. . . all that is in the Heavens and the earth glorifieth God. And the birds in flight—each one knoweth its prayer and way of glorification' (24:41).

Sūrat al-Takāthur (102)

Rivalry in Worldly Increase
In the Name of God, the Compassionate, the Merciful

[102:1]
Rivalry in worldly increase distracteth you
[102:2]
Until ye come to the graves.
[102:3]
Nay, but ye will come to know!
[102:4]
Nay, but ye will come to know!
[102:5]
Nay, would that ye knew (now) with a sure knowledge!
[102:6]
For ye will behold hell-fire.
[102:7]
Aye, ye will behold it with sure vision.
[102:8]
Then, on that day, ye will be asked concerning pleasure.

* * *

The clear spiritual warning in this *Sūra* is to guard oneself against worldliness, both materially and overtly—competing with others in terms of greedy acquisition of material things of this world—and subtly and covertly—seeking increase in renown, praise, prestige or power. The word *takāthur* derives from a root meaning abundance, but in this context the abundance being sought—and being sought competitively, in relation to others, as indicated by the reciprocity of the verbal form taken here, *tafāʿul*—is clearly of the egotistical and materialistic order. This, in contrast to the other *Sūra* of the Qurʾan in which this root is found, namely, *Sūrat al-Kawthar*, the abundance of which relates, on the one hand, to the plenitude of Paradise symbolised by the celestial pool named al-Kawthar, and to the prefiguration of that celestial grace in the person of Fāṭima, as will be seen in the discussion below on this *Sūra*.

One is being urged in this short *Sūra* to rid oneself of the worldliness, overt and subtle, which obscures the eye of the heart from knowledge of that which is certain, namely: death, judgement and life Hereafter. A certain knowledge of the ineluctability of death ought to be sufficient to dissolve the vices of greed and selfishness in the soul. However, these vices, if not recognised, opposed and overcome, will conversely prevent the knowledge in question from arising in the soul. The Prophet said: 'Remember much that which ends all pleasures (*hādhim al-ladhdhāt*): Death.'[33]

One is urged to die to worldliness before the world 'dies', as it does for you, when you are snatched from it. Spiritual detachment stands forth as the antidote to material attachment: the former leads to eternal life in the spirit, the latter leads to destruction in the perishable world of matter.

As regards the 'knowledge of certainty' and the 'eye of certainty', these are crucially related to the vision of the heart, and thus to the spiritual quest. These phrases evoke the Qur'ānic injunction: 'And worship thy Lord until certainty come unto thee' (15:99). It is worship, devotion, and its quintessence, the remembrance of God (*dhikr Allāh*), which generates certainty. One of Imam 'Alī's most famous statements is: 'Were the veil to be lifted, I could not be increased in certainty (*law kushifa'l-ghiṭā' mā azdadtu yaqīnan*)'.[34] In other words, such was the absolute nature of his certainty of ultimate reality that even if the veils of manifestation, of creation, of relativity be lifted, his certainty of the Absolute could not be made more absolute.

As regards the opening of the 'eye' of certainty, one should take careful note of the Imam's reply to Dhi'lib, when asked whether he had seen his Lord. 'I would not worship a Lord I had not seen!' the Imam said. When asked how he saw Him, the Imam replied: 'Eyes see Him not according to outward vision, but hearts see Him according to the spiritual realities of faith (*lā tudrikuhu'l-'uyūn bi-mushāhadati'l-'iyān, wa lākin tudrikuhu'l-qulūb bi-ḥaqā'iq al-īmān*)'.[35]

In another saying the Imam refers to 'pure hearts' as the 'places' from where God can be seen, 'so whoever purifies his heart sees God (*Qulūb al-'ibād al-ṭāhira mawāḍi'u naẓari'Llāh, fa-man ṭahhara qalbahu naẓara ilayhi*)'.[36] The relationship between the purification of the heart and the remembrance of God is affirmed in this saying: 'Where are they whose actions are accomplished purely for God, and who purify their hearts [so that they become] places for the remembrance of God?'[37] The 'eye' of certainty is thus at one with the 'eye' of the heart, which is enabled to 'see' God by the spiritual realities of faith—certainty and gnosis—thanks to the remembrance of God, described by the Imam as *afḍal al-ʿibāda*, 'the most excellent form of worship'. The spiritual quest for the vision of God, for the opening of the eye of the heart, for the participation in 'knowledge of certainty' is thus bound up with the 'remembrance of God'. As was seen in the discussion of *Sūrat al-Aʿlā*, the remembrance of God is described as a 'polish for hearts', enabling the heart to see after being blind. The fact that this comment is made on a verse connected to the famous *Āyat al-nūr* ('verse of light') means that the Imam is also commenting, implicitly, on that verse. The heart needs to be 'polished' by the *dhikr*, so that it can come to 'see' God according to the 'spiritual realities of faith', the 'eye of certainty' and arrive at the 'knowledge of certainty'; the heart can only 'see' God's light by virtue of the presence of that light already within the heart, but the light is obscured by the clouds of forgetfulness, egotism and vice, whence the need for the *dhikr*:

> God is the light of the heavens and the earth. A similitude of His light is a niche wherein is a lamp; the lamp is enclosed in a glass; the glass is as it were a shining star. [The lamp] is lit by [the oil of] a blessed olive tree, neither of the East nor of the West. The oil well-nigh shineth forth, though fire touch it not. Light upon light! God guideth to His light whom He will; and God striketh similitudes for mankind; and God knoweth all things (24:35).

Just as the Imams—and all true saints, the *awliyāʾ Allāh*, 'friends of God'—are themselves the embodiments of light, reflections of the Light of God—'light upon light'—so they teach mankind how to bring to light this spiritual knowledge within themselves. The *dhikr* is the very cornerstone of the method taught by the Imams to their followers in the spiritual quest. It is for this reason that, whereas all other acts of devotion are fixed as regards time and place and frequency, there is no limit whatsoever that can be placed on the *dhikr*. As Imam Jaʿfar al-Ṣādiq says: 'Everything has a limit, at which it terminates, except the *dhikr Allāh*. God has made obligatory the religious duties (*al-farā'iḍ*), so whoever fulfils them, that fulfilment constitutes their limit. For the month of Ramaḍān, whoever fasts therein, that constitutes its limit . . .' He proceeds to mention other rites, and then cites the Qur'ānic verse: 'O ye who believe, invoke God with much invocation' (33:41), and adds that his father, Imam Muḥammad al-Bāqir, never ceased invoking, even while eating and walking.[38]

This reminds one of the verse in the Qur'ān in which the 'possessors of substance' (*ūlu'l-albāb*) are described, those who combine perpetual invocation with profound reflection: 'Truly in the creation of the heavens and the earth, and in the alternation between night and day, there are signs for those of substance, those who invoke God standing, sitting and reclining on their sides, and reflect upon the creation of the heavens and the earth . . .' (3:190–191). Finally, let us note this extraordinary saying pertaining to the *dhikr*, a saying of the Prophet which reveals the gulf between conventional religiosity and uncompromising spirituality: 'Increase the *dhikru'Llāh* until they call you a madman (*majnūn*)!'[39]

Sūrat al-ʿAṣr (103)

The Declining Day
In the Name of God, the Compassionate, the Merciful

[103:1]
By the declining day,
[103:2]
Indeed, man is in a state of loss,
[103:3]
Save those who believe and perform virtuous deeds, and exhort one another to truth and exhort one another to patience.

* * *

The contemporary Shiʿi commentator, Makārim Shīrāzī writes: 'Such is the comprehensiveness of this *Sūra* that certain exegetes have claimed that all of the different forms of knowledge and all the ultimate aims of the Qur'ān are summarised within it.'[40]

It might also be said that the goal of the spiritual quest is contained within the description of the believers as being those who practise virtue, and who urge one another to truth and to patience. For in these four elements—faith, virtue, truth and patience—one has the quintessential portrait of the Prophet of Islam, and it is this emulation of the fine and beautiful example (*uswa ḥasana*; 33:21) which constitutes the foundation and the goal of the spiritual quest.

One should note two polarities in the four elements stressed in this chapter: the two elements, truth (*al-ḥaqq*) and patience (*al-ṣabr*) are related to faith and virtue respectively: truth is the supreme object of faith, and patience can be seen to sum up all the virtues. Patience combined with truth produces that quality which defines the Prophetic character so well: *ḥilm*, a term which one can translate into English only by using several concordant terms: wisdom, gentleness, tolerance, patience, self-composure, compassion, far-sightedness, magnanimity and equanimity. The virtue of patience, then, is not to be confined simply to the notion of endurance, of putting up with a difficult situation. It is to be understood in light of its divine archetype, *al-Ṣabūr*, the Infinitely Patient. God's 'patience' is obviously not to be understood in terms resembling human patience; on the contrary, it is human patience which must reflect the divine archetype of this quality. At the divine level, patience is a quality which cannot be disassociated from all of the other qualities, and in particular, knowledge, which render patience possible. For human patience to reflect the divine quality, therefore, it must be infused with knowledge of ultimate reality: believers must 'exhort one another to truth', first, and then 'exhort one another to patience'. Patience flows spontaneously in the light of the truth, whereas impatience, aggression and violence spring from the opposite: error and ignorance. The *jāhil* is not simply one who is 'ignorant', even though this is its primary meaning; the *jāhil* is defined more fully as one whose ignorance leads him to act in an aggressive, irascible, proud manner. The opposite of the *jāhil* is not the *'alīm* (the knower) but the *ḥalīm*, the wise, gentle, compassionate and restrained person, exemplified to perfection by the Prophet.

Sūrat al-Quraysh (106)

The Quraysh
In the Name of God, the Compassionate, the Merciful

[106:1]
For the uniting of Quraysh.
[106:2]
For their uniting [We cause] the caravans to set forth in winter and summer.
[106:3]
So let them worship the Lord of this House,
[106:4]
Who hath fed them against hunger, and made them safe from fear.

* * *

This *Sūra* can be related to the spritual quest by every person who is aware that he or she has received the blessings of sustenance and of security, and who therefore knows that their worship is their principal means of manifesting gratitude. The 'House' is, outwardly, the Kaʿba, and inwardly can be taken to represent the heart. The heart has been protected by its Lord against the insecurities of doubt, fear of death, and has been fed by the nourishing sustenance of certainty and virtue. The Quraysh can stand for the various faculties of the soul;[41] all the diverse and often competing elements of the soul have been united around the Kaʿba of the heart. The unification of the tribe signifies totality of soul, and this totality of soul is the prerequisite for the sincerity and authenticity of worship.

Sūrat al-Māʿūn (107)

Small Kindnesses
In the Name of God, the Compassionate, the Merciful

[107:1]
Hast thou observed him who belieth religion?
[107:2]
That is he who repelleth the orphan,
[107:3]
And urgeth not the feeding of the needy.
[107:4]
So woe unto worshippers
[107:5]
Who are heedless of their prayer;
[107:6]
Who would be seen [at worship]
[107:7]
Yet refuse small kindnesses!

* * *

It is recorded that this censure of religious hypocrisy was directed at the hypocrites who had entered Islam only superficially, and who made a show of their adherence to the faith, but belied it in their lack of charity to orphans and beggars.[42] It has a wider significance as regards the spiritual quest, in that it underlines the integral role played by charity in the articulation of one's faith. Those who have true faith are described in connection with the 'steep ascent' (*al-ʿaqaba*) in the *Sūrat al-Balad*:

Yet he hath not embarked upon the steep ascent.
And what will show thee what the steep ascent is?
It is the freeing of a slave,
Or feeding on a day of hunger,
An orphan near of kin,

Or a needy one in desolation;
And to be of those who believe, and exhort one another to
patience and to compassion (90:11–17).

Faith, patience and compassion thus go hand in hand and are expressed outwardly by the acts mentioned, but embrace the whole range of charitable acts which one can perform. The integrity and the authenticity of one's prayer is thus inextricable from virtue. Without the practice of virtue, one's formal worship is deprived of sincerity, it is thus that one who prays, and is heedless of his prayers, is described as one who belies religion, who violates the integrity of *al-dīn*, insofar as he ruptures the nexus between faith and virtue. Religion is that by means of which the symbiosis between faith, articulated by worship, and virtue, most tangibly manifested as generosity, is sustained and deepened. Without worship, the practice of virtue may well be deprived of humility—one's charity might serve to intensify one's pride. Conversely, those who pray 'only to be seen at prayer' are not truly praying; and they betray their pretentiousness by their lack of virtue. The implication for the spiritual quest here is this: the sincerity or purity of one's worship will be deepened in the measure of one's inner intention to be generous, compassionate and virtuous in all respects. The practice of these virtues, in turn, helps to eliminate those elements of hypocrisy or ostentation which may still be tainting one's worship, if not overtly, then in the form of subtle egotism and secret self-satisfaction.

Imam 'Alī refers to the dangers of religious pretension—showing off one's piety—as *shirk*, polytheism, helping one to see why the Qur'ān refers to the hypocrites as those who 'belie' the religion of Islam: 'Know that the slightest pretension (*riyā'*) is polytheism.'[43] The verses in this chapter, and indeed all of the verses of the Qur'ān which inveigh against the hypocrites, can be interpreted as warnings to those elements within one's own soul which tend to place more importance on the outward display of piety and virtue than on nourishing their inner substance for the sake of God. *Tawḥīd*, on this level, implies being virtuous 'vertically', for God; *shirk*, on this same level, implies the desire to be virtuous 'horizontally', for the sake of ostentatious display to others, and to one's own ego, which can secretly take pride in this show of virtue.

Sūrat al-Kawthar (108)

Abundance
In the Name of God, the Compassionate, the Merciful

[108:1]
Truly, We have given thee Abundance;
[108:2]
So pray unto thy Lord, and sacrifice.
[108:3]
Truly, it is thy insulter who is without posterity.

* * *

This is the shortest of all the *Sūras* of the Qur'ān. Several interpretations of the meaning of the word 'Kawthar' are given by the commentators, among the most commonly cited are the following: abundant good (the most literal meaning); the Qur'ān itself; a pool or river or fountain in Paradise; wisdom.[44] In addition to these, all Shi'i commentators refer to the interpretation of the word according to which it comes to mean the abundant progeny granted to the Prophet through his daughter Fāṭima. This interpretation is borne out by the remainder of the *Sūra*, in which the 'enemy' of the Prophet is called *al-abtar*, the one who has no posterity. For this was the insulting epithet by which the Prophet was known after the death of his baby son, 'Abd Allāh; those who had no sons in the culture of that time were insulted by this name. The Prophet is told that he has indeed a rich progeny, and that by contrast his detractors are the ones who are in reality fruitless.

This interpretation has considerable significance for the spiritual quest: to the extent that one is aware that one has received the abundant good embodied in the Prophetic gifts—the Qur'ān itself, the wisdom of Prophetic guidance—one can only pray and sacrifice, as a manifestation of one's gratitude. One no longer prays only that one might be given some good in this world, or the next, but one prays out of gratitude for what has already been given, here and now. As noted earlier, Imam 'Alī refers to this kind of worship as being the worship of those who are 'free': 'Indeed there is a group who worship God out of desire [for something not yet attained]; and this is the worship of the merchants. And there is a group who worship God out of fear, and this is the worship of the enslaved. And there is a group who worship God out of gratitude, and this is the worship of the free.' The Prophet, upon being asked why he persisted with such long prayer vigils through the night, replied by saying: 'Am I not a grateful servant?'[45]

Sūrat al-Naṣr (110)

Succour
In the Name of God, the Compassionate, the Merciful

[110:1]
When God's succour and the triumph cometh
[110:2]
And when thou seest mankind entering the religion of God in droves
[110:3]
Then hymn the praises of thy Lord and seek forgiveness of Him. Truly, He is ever ready to show mercy.

* * *

As regards the theme of the spiritual quest, this short *Sūra* is significant in pointing to the perpetual need on the part of the soul to glorify God and to seek forgiveness—even in the midst of so great a worldly victory as that granted to the Prophet over his detractors. However great be the external trappings of success, one's spiritual success resides in ceaselessly praising God for whatever success has been granted, doing so in the full knowledge that there is no success or triumph except through the grace of God: 'There is no victory except through God, the Mighty, the Wise' (3:126; repeated almost verbatim at 8:10). This being the case, there can be no cause for self-congratulation when one achieves any success, whether material or spiritual. Rather, one is reminded of the need to remain humble in the face of the graces bestowed by God, and to seek forgiveness for the inevitable imperfections of soul which remain, however great be the spiritual success granted by God. One's seeking of forgiveness, in the measure of its sincerity, will always be granted, however, given that 'He is ever ready to show mercy' (*innahu kāna tawwāban*). However great be one's shortcomings, one never allows oneself to fall into despair in the spiritual life, given that God forgives all sins. As cited earlier: 'O My slaves, ye who have been extravagant to the detriment of your souls, despair not of the mercy of God. Truly God forgiveth all sins; He is indeed the Forgiving, the Merciful' (39:53). The ultimate 'triumph' is to enter into the embrace of divine mercy both in this life and in the Hereafter:

> Those [angels] who bear the Throne, and all who are around it, hymn the praises of their Lord and believe in Him, and seek forgiveness for those who believe, [saying:] Our Lord, Thou encompassest all things in mercy and knowledge, so forgive those who repent and follow Thy path, and protect them from the pain of hell. Our Lord, admit them into the Gardens of Eden which Thou hast promised them, together with those of their forefathers and spouses and descendants who were righteous. Truly Thou art the Mighty, the Wise. And protect them against all evil deeds; those whom Thou protectest against [the consequences of] evil deeds on that Day, they are truly those unto whom Thou hast been merciful. That is the supreme triumph (40:7–9).

Sūrat al-Ikhlāṣ (112)

Unity
In the Name of God, the Compassionate, the Merciful

[112:1]
Say: He is God, the One!
[112:2]
God, the eternally Besought of all!
[112:3]
He begetteth not, nor was begotten.
[112:4]
Nor hath He any equal.

* * *

The two key principles of *ikhlāṣ* ('sincerity/purity') and *tawḥīd* ('integrating oneness') are expressed in this chapter in the most succinct manner possible. The Prophet referred to this *Sūra* as being the equivalent of one-third of the entire Qur'ān, according to the following report. He asked his companions: 'Are any of you incapable of reciting one third of the Qur'ān in a single night?' Upon being asked who could perform such a feat, he replied simply: 'Recite [the Sūra] beginning *Qul huwa'Llāhu aḥad*.'[46]

In sermon number 108 of the *Nahj al-balāgha*[47] Imam 'Alī alludes to this Sūra when speaking about the 'word of sincerity' (*kalimatu'l-ikhlāṣ*), which is understood also to refer to the first testimony of Islam, *lā ilāha illa'Llāh*, this testimony being the 'purest' expression of *tawḥīd*. This equation between the *Sūrat al-Ikhlāṣ* and the formula of *tawḥīd* underlines the foundational nature of this *Sūra*. In this sermon, the Imam describes it simply as *al-fiṭra*, the primordial nature of man, thereby showing the relationship between the assertion of the oneness of God and the comprehension of the oneness of humanity implied in this *Sūra*.

In his letter to Mālik al-Ashtar, the Imam makes this unity of the human race explicit, together with the imperative of compassion; here, the Imam shows that compassion is both cause and consequence of this vision of the oneness of humanity. On the one hand, compassion is the ethical expression of this spiritual recognition of the oneness of all human beings; and on the other, it is the chief means by which one can arrive at this vision of the oneness of all humanity:

> Infuse your heart with mercy for the subjects, love for them and kindness towards them. Be not like a ravenous beast of prey above them, seeking to devour them. For they are of two types: either your brother in religion or your equal in creation. Mistakes slip from them, defects emerge from them, deliberately or accidentally. So bestow upon them your forgiveness and your pardon, just as you would have God bestow upon you His forgiveness and pardon; for you are above them, and the one who appointed you as governor is above you, and God is above him who appointed you.[48]

Another verse of the Qur'ān expresses this aspect of total dedication called for in the spiritual quest for *ikhlāṣ*, pure, all-embracing sincerity: 'Truly my worship and my sacrifice, and my living and my dying, are for God, Lord of the worlds' (6:162).

The following words of Imam ʿAlī can be read as a comment on this verse, and on the principle of *ikhlāṣ*, containing as they do a direct reference to the verbal form of the word: 'Make purely for God (*akhliṣ li'Llāh*) your action and your knowledge, your love and your hatred, your taking and your leaving, your speech and your silence.'[49] The quest for this *ikhlāṣ* is thus a quest for a total integration of the soul—a 'making one'—which is the reflection on the human plane of that oneness of God on the transcendent plane. As the Imam says elsewhere: 'He who knows God integrates himself (*man ʿarafa'Llāh tawaḥḥad*).'[50] The knowledge of divine oneness, in its totality and all its depth, flows forth only in the measure that the soul itself is one, that is, insofar as it has been subjected to the process of sincere unification (*tawaḥḥud*). To be 'sincere' implies an effort to give oneself to God with all that one is, leaving nothing out; it implies ridding oneself of all impurity, hypocrisy, egotism; it implies that one make an effort to be totally dominated by the vision of the divine unity, and in consequence of this, the vision of the oneness of the human race. By means of this vision of the oneness of humanity, one is enabled to bring oneself into harmony with all other human beings, and thereby with the primordial nature of humanity as such, *al-fiṭra.*

The absolute oneness of God also relates to the spiritual quest in that the words 'there is nothing like unto Him' bear a deep esoteric message: there is no 'other' in existence, God alone is real, in the ultimate sense. This esoteric aspect of the oneness of God takes us from the simple numerical conception of divine unity—there is but one God, not many gods—to the more subtle recognition that, in the words of Imam 'Alī, 'that which has no second does not enter the category of number'. This is not a oneness which can be counted, rather, it is a oneness which embraces the whole of reality: there is 'nothing like unto Him', because there is nothing apart from Him. Here, it is a question of spiritual vision and not simple theological reasoning: one is called upon to recognise that 'wherever ye turn, there is the Face of God' (2:115), this being one of the most challenging and rewarding aspects of the spiritual quest for ultimate reality: to see the manifestations of God everywhere, while knowing that His Essence remains forever invisible and ineffable.

In his commentary on this chapter Kāshānī cites the famous words of Imam 'Alī from the first sermon of the *Nahj al-balāgha*: 'As the Commander of the Faithful—upon whom be peace—says: "The perfection of *ikhlāṣ* in regard to Him is to divest Him of all Attributes—because of the testimony of every Attribute that it is other than the object of attribution, and because of the testimony of every such object that it is other than the Attribute."'

Kāshānī deems this apophatic statement of Imam 'Alī, apparently denuding God of all Attributes, to be the perfect way of removing 'all stain of multiplicity from the one reality'. But, one might ask, what becomes of the multiplicity which is within God, that multiplicity constituted by the divine Attributes named throughout the Qur'ān?[51] Imam 'Alī would, of course, uphold the reality of these Attributes, but each of them is defined, earlier in the first sermon, as having no determinable limit (*laysa li-ṣifatihi ḥadd maḥdūd*). In other words, each Attribute is identical to the Essence, and can be distinguished from it only from a relative point of view: the full rigour of the meaning of God's exclusive oneness (*aḥadiyya*) can only be grasped if this relative point of view is negated.[52] So what is being negated is not, and cannot be, the Attributes as such; what is negated can only be the ontological validity of our conception of those Attributes. Our conception of the Attributes is utterly transcended by the unfathomable reality of those Attributes as they are in themselves; because what they are in themselves—ontologically—is nothing other than the Essence of God. In this manner the unimpeachable oneness of God is maintained, in the very bosom of a simultaneous affirmation and negation of the Attributes; an affirmation of them as being nothing but the Essence, and a negation of them insofar as they are fashioned—and thereby relativised—by our conception of them as distinct, discrete, separate entities. There is only one 'entity', or real Being, and that is the divine Oneness: 'Say: God is One.' As mentioned above, this oneness is not to be simplistically subsumed by the category of number: 'that which has no second does not enter the category of number'.

The oneness in question is therefore metaphysical and ontological, not conceptual and numerical. Even if, on the relative plane of concepts and number, it is the notion of oneness which most adequately symbolises the supreme Reality, what Imam 'Alī is implying in his apophatic statements is that this notion of 'oneness' remains, after all, a symbol, and must not be crudely equated with the reality symbolised. On the supra-conceptual and metaphysical plane, that of objective Being, the oneness in question is intuited as both all-exclusive—excluding all relativity, hence all multiplicity—and all-inclusive, hence containing within itself all multiplicity: for 'that which has no second' must perforce include all things within itself. It includes 'all things' not as discrete ontologically distinct entities, but insofar as their divine substance is concerned; this substance is referred to as the *arkān*, 'foundations' or 'pillars', in a verse from the *Du'ā' Kumayl* in which Imam 'Alī refers to the 'Names' of God 'which have filled the foundations of all things'.[53]

The vision of unity which unfolds here is one in which all outward multiplicity is integrated by virtue of the multiplicity of the divine Names and Attributes; these Attributes are then conceptually negated in order to be ontologically integrated. They are integrated within the One, and this One demands that its dimension of transcendent exclusivity be combined with that of its immanent inclusivity if our conception of divine oneness is to be an adequate symbol or reflection of that oneness. God as 'the One', *al-Aḥad*, excludes all things in ineffable transcendence; but God is also described by such names as 'the All-Encompassing', *al-Muḥīṭ*, which, by virtue of encompassing all things, includes them all in its unfathomable immanence. Similarly, divine knowledge and mercy are described as all-encompassing: 'Thou hast encompassed all things by mercy and knowledge.' If our conception of God is to do justice to these mysteries it must be capable not only of combining these antinomies and paradoxes, but more importantly, the mind must grasp the incommensurability between its own subjective conceptions of 'oneness' and that oneness per se, that is, such as this oneness is objectively, in and of itself: between human knowledge and divine Reality there is a chasm which can be bridged only by the extinction of the human in the bosom of the divine. The spiritual purpose of this conceptual negation of multiplicity, then, is to pave the way for the extinction (*fanāʾ*) of relativity and the subsistence (*baqāʾ*) of Reality. This is mirrored in the first testimony of Islam: the negation, *lā ilāha*, must precede, logically and ontologically, the affirmation, *illaʾLlāh*.

What the Imam says about the 'perfection' and reality of the remembrance of God (*dhikr Allāh*) is relevant here:

> Do not remember God absent-mindedly (*sāhiyan*), nor forget Him in distraction; rather, remember Him with perfect remembrance (*dhikran kāmilan*), a remembrance in which your heart and tongue are in harmony, and what you conceal conforms with what you reveal. But you will not remember Him according to the true reality of the remembrance (*ḥaqīqat al-dhikr*) until you forget your own soul in your remembrance.[54]

Insofar as one's individual consciousness is present, God cannot be 'remembered', invoked, still less, known; when individuality—hence, relativity and multiplicity—is effaced from consciousness, then does consciousness rejoin its true nature: consciousness shorn of individuality is akin to divine oneness shorn of multiplicity, for it is on the basis of the inescapable relativity of individual cognition that the Attributes of God appear to be multiple. Upon the extinction of individual cognition in the reality of the remembrance there arises a spiritual vision of the subsistence of the oneness of God beyond all formal multiplicity and beyond all numerical conceptions of unity. Once this vision of the Face of God is attained, above and beyond all phenomena, then that same Face reveals itself within and through all phenomena:

'Wherever ye turn, there is the Face of God' (2:115). In this light, one sees more clearly the depth of meaning behind the apparently simple negation of the Christian dogma of sonship: 'He begetteth not nor was begotten. Nor hath He any equal.'[55] He neither begets nor manifests anything that is 'other', nor can He be begotten or arise from an 'other', nor is anything equal to Him—for the simple reason that nothing other than Him exists: He is 'that which has no second'. Everything that appears to be other than Him is in reality a manifestation of one dimension of His own Reality, one aspect of His Face; the multiplicity of these manifestations are not other than the One, they do not render the One multiple, nor do they add anything to the One: their outward multiplicity simply reflects the inner infinity of the One. And the reflection has no reality apart from that which it reflects. In this manner one can see that wherever one may look, 'there is the Face of God', for there is nothing in existence which is not, in one way or another, to one degree or another, a reflection of the one and only reality, the one and only 'Face' of God.

Sūrat al-Falaq (113)

The Daybreak
In the Name of God, the Compassionate, the Merciful

[113:1]
Say: I seek refuge in the Lord of the Daybreak
[113:2]
From the evil of that which He created;
[113:3]
From the evil of the darkness when it is intense,
[113:4]
And from the evil of malignant witchcraft,
[113:5]
And from the evil of the envier when he envieth.

* * *

The first thing to note about this chapter is that the evils from which one seeks refuge in God are the evils 'of that which He created', and not the evils 'which He created'. One is not ascribing directly to God the creation of evil. One is seeking refuge in His absolute goodness from the evils which derive from the negation of that goodness, the evils which arise out of the created order. Just as in the case of the *Fātiḥa*, where anger is not directly ascribed to God at verse 7, so in this verse, the creation of negative phenomena are not directly ascribed to God, only the creation as such is. The seeking of divine protection against the evils of creation can also be appreciated microcosmically, these evils being grasped as so many tendencies of one's own soul; this sharpens our perception of what needs to be fought against in the 'greater holy war', *al-jihād al-akbar*, the war against one's own vices, failings and errors. In particular, seeking protection against the 'evil of the envier when he envies', can be seen as both an external vice and an internal one: the soul must make an effort to seek that grace which liberates it from the prison of envy, conscious or otherwise. One is tempted to attribute to oneself purity and an absence of envy, but the Qur'ān warns against such complacency, and challenges the soul to address its own failings and not ignore or minimise them: 'So ascribe not purity unto yourselves' (53:32); 'We verily created man, and We know what his soul whispereth to him' (50:16). The whispering in question is one of the themes of the following *Sūra*.

The relationship between the evils outside oneself and the receptivity to evil within the soul is made explicit in another verse of the Qur'ān: 'Shall I tell upon whom the demons descend? They descend on every sinful liar' (26:221–222). Were it not for one's sinful propensities, the demons would have no possibility of influencing the soul: 'I had no power over you,' Satan says, to those who fell prey to his promises, 'all I did was call out to you, and ye responded to me. So blame me not, blame but yourselves' (14:23). The demonic insinuations are kept at bay by seeking refuge in God, as indicated in this *Sūra*; and the principal means of taking refuge is to precipitate oneself into a state of recollectedness before God, remembering the divine presence, and invoking the Name of God, as one is urged to do in the Qur'ān: 'If a temptation from Satan disturbs thee, seek refuge in God. He is the Hearer, the Knower. When the pious are subjected to an insinuation of Satan, they remember God, and behold: they can perceive [clearly again]' (7:200–201). Those who are immune to demonic insinuations and from evil promptings within are described as the 'slaves' of God: Satan promises to 'beguile' each and every soul, except the purified, sincere slaves of God (38:82–83). The same message is delivered in the following dialogue between Satan and God:

> He (Satan) said: 'My Lord, because Thou hast sent me astray, I verily shall adorn evil for them in the earth, and shall mislead every one of them—except thy purified, sincere slaves ...' [God said:] 'You have no power over My slaves—[you have power] only over those who go astray and follow you' (15:39–42).

And again:

> Satan hath no power over those who believe and trust in their Lord. His power is only exercised over those who befriend him, and those who ascribe partners unto Him (16:100).

These verses show that those who fully believe, and who trust absolutely in the Lord are the 'purified, sincere slaves'. These slaves in turn are described in the *Sūrat al-Insān*, cited and discussed above, in reference specifically to the Ahl al-Bayt. It is they who embody to perfection the qualities of 'slavehood', but the qualities themselves can be cultivated and realised by all those whose spiritual quest is sincere and serious.

Another key verse which reinforces the equation between the Imams and those effaced 'slaves' of God over whom Satan has no authority is the verse which declares that God has utterly purified the Ahl al-Bayt: 'Truly God only wishes to remove from you all impurity, O Ahl al-Bayt, and to purify you with a complete purification' (33:33). It is thanks to this purity that the Ahl al-Bayt can be followed as perfect exemplars, devoid of egotism, and by that very fact, rendered transparent to the light of *walāya* which flows through them, from the divine realm to the human order. They have overcome the 'darkness of the veil of egotism' as well as any sinful propensity, the sole bases upon which Satan can gain mastery over human beings. All those who follow the path leading to the effacement of egotism and the negation of all sinful propensity within them can thus enter into the safety of 'slavehood', and be rendered immune to the insinuations and promptings of external forces of evil, whether in the form of human beings, jinns or demons. This theme—*wiswās*, or whispering—continues in the following chapter.

Sūrat al-Nās (114)

Mankind
In the Name of God, the Compassionate, the Merciful

[114:1]
Say: I seek refuge in the Lord of mankind,
[114:2]
The King of mankind,
[114:3]
The God of mankind,
[114:4]
From the evil of the sneaking whisperer,
[114:5]
Who whispereth in the hearts of mankind,
[114:6]
Of the jinn and of mankind.

* * *

Before continuing with the discussion of *wiswās* from the previous *Sūra*, it is important to stress the repetition of the word *nās* at the end of the first three verses, and then again at the end of the final two verses. In other words, it is only verse 4 which does not contain this key word which gives the *Sūra* its name. The unity of the human race is therefore one of the most important themes of this chapter: humanity is, as stressed in the first three verses, utterly dominated by the 'Lord' of mankind (*rabb al-nās*), the 'King' of mankind (*malik al-nās*), the 'God' of mankind (*ilāh al-nās*). Just as the one God takes on different names and qualities in relation to humanity, while remaining nonetheless the selfsame divinity, likewise, humanity is one substance, while nonetheless assuming a multitude of races, ethnicities, colours, cultures and languages. Thus, such verses as the following are evoked by this repeated emphasis on *al-nās*: 'O mankind, truly We have created you male and female, and have made you nations and tribes that ye may know one another. Truly the most noble of you, in the sight of

God, is the most pious of you. Truly, God is Knowing, Aware' (49:13). This verse underlines the absolute spiritual equality between all people, irrespective of gender, tribe, or nation: it is piety alone, whatever be the group to which one belongs, that determines one's worth as a human being in the eyes of God.

Other key verses to be borne in mind in relation to the emphasis on *al-nās* are the following:

> And among His signs is that He created you from dust, then when you attain to humanity, you spread diversely. And among His signs is that He created for you spouses from your own souls, that ye might find repose in them; and he placed between you love and mercy. Indeed, herein are signs for those who reflect. And of His signs is the creation of the heavens and the earth, and the differences of your languages and colours. Indeed, herein are signs for those who know (30:20–22).

Such verses as these help to clarify the meaning of *al-nās*, all mankind, as one integrated whole, despite the multitude of distinctions between them; this is a human reflection of the Lord who governs them, the one and only Lord, who remains One, despite assuming a multitude of Names and Qualities.

Returning to the theme of *wiswās*, discussed in relation to the previous *Sūra*: one seeks refuge in God from the whispering of the enemy, which is to be grasped not only as an external foe, but as the promptings of one's own lower nature, the impulses of one's own egotism, vanity, desire, caprice—all of which are summed up in the Qur'ān by the single word *hawā*. We are asked: 'Hast thou seen him who maketh his desire (*hawā*) his god?' (25:43; almost identical at 45:23). The greatest weapon in this spiritual battle against the false god of one's own *hawā* is consciousness of God, and, in consequence of this consciousness, self-restraint, as indicated in these verses: 'As for him who feareth the station of his Lord, and restraineth his soul from desire (*hawā*), verily, Paradise will be his abode' (79:40–41).

The soul, although 'created in the finest stature', has been brought down by its own forgetfulness to be 'the lowest of the low' (97:4–5); it is for this reason that we are told 'truly the soul inciteth unto evil—unless my Lord hath mercy' (12:53). It is by means of the remembrance of God that one opens oneself up to this merciful deliverance from the incitements of one's own soul. The soul characterised by evil promptings (*al-nafs al-ammāra*) is transformed into 'the self-accusing soul' (*al-nafs al-lawwāma*; 75:2) once the 'greater spiritual struggle' has begun, and one is truly fighting against one's *hawā*. Imam 'Alī gives us a vivid image of this greatest of all battles, whereby the intellect is the leader of the forces of *al-Raḥmān*; and *al-hawā* commands the forces of *al-shayṭān* (the devil). The soul itself is described as 'susceptible to the attraction of both' (*mutajādhiba baynahumā*) and enters into 'the domain of whichever of the two will triumph'.[56]

The soul is won over for al-Raḥmān only when, through the realisation of truth and the perfection of virtue, it attains the quality of *iṭmiʾnān*, 'peace in certainty'; the soul that is now qualified as *al-nafs al-muṭmaʾinna* is addressed in words already quoted earlier, from the *Sūrat al-Fajr*: 'O thou soul which art at peace, return unto thy Lord with gladness that is thine in Him and His in thee; enter thou amongst my servants, enter My Garden' (89:27–30). As has been made clear, it is the remembrance of God which bestows this quality of *iṭmiʾnān* upon the soul, allowing it to achieve its goal in the spiritual quest, and be transformed from *al-nafs al-lawwāma* to *al-nafs al-muṭmaʾinna*. In the following verses the believers are described as 'those whose hearts are at peace through the remembrance of God' (*taṭmaʾinnu qulūbuhum bi-dhikri'Llāh*); 'is it not in the remembrance of God that hearts are at peace?' (13:28). It is for this reason, among others, that the Qurʾān says that, while the prayer keeps one away from 'indecency and evil', the remembrance of God is greater (*wa la-dhikru'Llāhi akbar*) (29:45).

Finally, it should be noted, in relation to the universal import of this *Sūra* with its repetition of *al-nās*, mankind, and of the One Lord who governs over all mankind, that the spiritual quest of each and every individual is integrally bound up with the whole of humanity. Whatever one achieves by way of changing oneself for the better, morally, intellectually and spiritually, has repercussions on all other souls, not only because 'Your creation and your resurrection [O mankind] are but as [the creation and resurrection of] a single soul' (31:28); but also because 'God changeth not the condition of a people until they change the condition of their own souls' (13:11). The sincere quest of each soul for God, and for self-realisation in God, is thus far from being an egotistical exercise; on the contrary, the effort of each person to change for the better the condition of his or her soul redounds to the benefit of all human beings, doing so in accordance with the two principles of *tawḥīd* and *tawfīq*: that is, according to the unitive dynamics hidden within the spirit of *tawḥīd* which, on the human plane, renders all souls as one; and in harmony with the irresistible rhythms of *tawfīq*, divine grace, which responds to every sincere prayer:

> And when My servants question thee about Me, [tell them] I am indeed near. I answer the supplication of the suppliant when he calleth unto Me. So let them answer Me, and let them trust in Me, in order that they may be led aright (2:186).

Notes

Introduction

1 *The Scale of Wisdom: A Compendium of Shi'a Hadith* (translation of Muḥammadī Rayshahrī's compilation, *Mīzān al-ḥikma*), ed. N. Virjee (London, 2009), p. 900.
2 For discussion of this universal aspect of the Qur'ānic message see Reza Shah-Kazemi, *The Other in the Light of the One: The Universality of the Qur'an and Interfaith Dialogue* (Cambridge, 2006).
3 Reflecting upon these verses urging us to reflect would in itself constitute a most rewarding meditation; the verses in which this type of reflection—that is, employing the form *tafakkara* only—are: 2:219; 2:266; 3:191; 6:50; 7:176; 7:184; 10:24; 13:3; 16:11; 16:44; 16:69; 30:8; 30:21; 34:46; 39:42; 45:13; 59:21.
4 It should be noted that this fifth form of the verb (*tafa''ala/tafa''ul*) strongly implies a dynamic motion, so that *tadabbur, tafaqquh, ta'ammul*, etc., are to be understood as so many aspects of a continuous effort of reflection, comprehension, contemplation; a continuous process of assimilation and realisation.
5 This calculation is based on the concordance of Fu'ād 'Abd al-Bāqī, ed., *al-Mu'jam al-mufahris li alfāẓ al-Qur'ān al-karīm* (Cairo, 1987). Franz Rosenthal correctly observes that *'ilm* is 'one of those concepts that have dominated Islam and given Muslim civilisation its distinctive shape and complexion. In fact, there is no other concept that has been operative as a determinant of Muslim civilisation in all its aspects to the same extent as *'ilm* . . . There is no branch of Muslim intellectual life, of Muslim religious and political life, and of the daily life of the average Muslim that remained untouched by the all-pervasive attitude towards "knowledge" as something of supreme value for Muslim being. *'Ilm* is Islam . . .'. F. Rosenthal, *Knowledge Triumphant: The Concept of Knowledge in Medieval Islam* (Leiden and Boston, 2007), p. 2.
6 *Ghurar al-ḥikam*, ed. Sayyid Ḥusayn Shaykh al-Islāmī (Qom, 2000), vol. 2, p. 970, no. 160 (all references to the *Ghurar* will be from this edition unless otherwise stated); as cited in Reza Shah-Kazemi, *Justice and Remembrance: Introducing the Spirituality of Imam 'Alī* (London, 2006), p. 49.
7 According to Ibn 'Abbās—and following him, the majority of Qur'ānic commentators—the word *ya'budūni* ('they worship Me') here means: *ya'rifūni* ('they know Me'), which is in harmony with Imam 'Alī's statement that there is no religion for one who has no intellect.
8 As cited in al-Qāḍī al-Nu'mān, *Da'ā'im al-Islām*, tr. Asaf A.A. Fyzee as *The Pillars of Islam* (New Delhi, 2002), vol. 1, p. 167.
9 Al-Ḥākim al-Nīsābūrī, *al-Mustadrak 'ala'l-ṣaḥīḥayn* (Beirut, 2002), p. 926, no. 4679.
10 *The Recitation and Interpretation of the Qur'ān: al-Ghazālī's Theory*, tr. M.

Abul Quasem (Kuala Lumpur, 1979), p. 63. This is a translation of Book 8 of al-Ghazālī's *Iḥyā' 'ulūm al-dīn.*

11 Al-Ghazālī, *Recitation*, p. 89.

12 *Nahj al-balāgha*, ed. Shaykh 'Azīzullāh al-'Uṭāridī (Tehran, 1993), Sermon 125, p. 144 (all references to the *Nahj* will be from this edition unless otherwise stated); as cited in Shah-Kazemi *Justice and Remembrance*, p. 25.

13 *Mawsū'at al-Imām 'Alī ibn Abī Ṭālib fi'l-kitāb wa'l-sunna wa'l-ta'rīkh*, ed. Muḥammad Rayshahrī (Qom, 1421/2000), vol. 8, p. 206.

14 Muḥammad Murādī, 'Rawish-i tafsīr-i Qur'ān' in 'Alī-Akbar Rashād, ed., *Dānish-nāmah-i Imām 'Alī* (Tehran, 2001), vol. 1, p. 237.

15 Murādī, 'Rawish-i tafsīr-i Qur'ān', pp. 238–239. Imam Ja'far al-Ṣādiq is also referred to as playing a foundational role in Qur'ānic exegesis, particularly as regards esoteric traditions of interpretation. According to Abdurrahman Habil, '. . . it was al-Ṣādiq who played the most important role in the whole history of esoteric commentaries upon the Qur'ān in both its Shī'ite and Sufi facets.' A. Habil, 'Traditional Esoteric Commentaries on the Quran', in Seyyed Hossein Nasr, ed., *Islamic Spirituality,* vol. 1, 'Foundations' (London, 1987), pp. 29–30.

16 *Scale of Wisdom*, p. 300.

17 *Ghurar*, vol. 2, p. 1222, no. 68.

18 The Qur'ān refers to its Arabic form in at least 10 verses; in addition to the three mentioned above, see 12:2, 13:37, 20:113, 39:28, 41:3, 42:7, 46:12. It is important to note the extraordinary extent to which the Arabic of the Qur'ān has fashioned a sense of religious unity among Muslims from the beginning of the Islamic period to our own times: whether the Muslim is in Morocco or Indonesia, Cape Town or Karachi, Tehran or London, differences of culture disappear as soon as he enters a mosque: for he is completely 'at home' as soon as the prayers begin to be recited in 'clear Arabic'.

19 Some western scholars of Islam are beginning to realise the importance of these untranslatable elements of the Qur'ān. See for example the fine chapter of Michael Sells, 'A Literary Approach to the Hymnic Sūras of the Qur'ān' in Issa Boullata, ed., *Literary Structures of Religious Meaning in the Qur'ān* (Richmond, 2000), pp. 3–25. What Sells refers to as 'aural intertextuality' is of particular interest. He defines this as: '1) the heightening of key acoustic features within a particular passage; 2) the connection of those sound features with key emotions, gender dynamics or semantic fields; 3) the forming of "sound figures" from this connection between acoustical features and a supple use of emotions, gender and semantics . . .; and 4) the intertextual play of such sound figures with similar or identical sound figures in other sūras' (p. 22).

20 Seyyed Hossein Nasr, 'Islam', in Arvind Sharma, ed., *Our Religions* (San Francisco, 1993), p. 448.

21 Muḥammad Ya'qūb al-Kulaynī, *al-Uṣūl min al-kāfī* (Tehran, 1376 Sh./1997), vol. 2, p. 608, no. 3518.

22 Kulaynī, *Uṣūl*, vol. 2, p. 608, no. 3519.

23 Kulaynī, *Uṣūl*, vol. 2, p. 607, no. 3514.

24 Frithjof Schuon expresses well the three aspects of the Qur'ān, doctrine, psychology and theurgy: 'These sources of metaphysical and eschatological doctrine, of mystical psychology and theurgic power lie hidden under a veil

of breathless utterances, often clashing in shock, of crystalline and fiery images, but also of passages majestic in rhythm, woven of every fibre of the human condition.' *Understanding Islam* (Bloomington, 1994), p. 46.

25 Cited in Shah-Kazemi, *Justice and Remembrance*, p. 119.

26 *Nahj al-balāgha*, tr. and ed. Ja'far Shahīdī (Tehran, 1378 Sh./1999), Sermon 147, p. 142.

27 *Nahj al-balāgha*, tr. and ed. Ja'far Shahīdī, Sermon 108, p. 100.

28 Later Sufi speculation, in harmony with this concordance, would distinguish between 'the creational Qur'ān' (*al-Qur'ān al-takwīnī*) and 'the written Qur'ān' (*al-Qur'ān al-tadwīnī*). The 14th-century Sufi 'Azīz al-Dīn Nasafī writes: 'Each day, destiny and the passage of time set this book before you, *sūrah* for *sūrah*, verse for verse, letter for letter and read it to you . . .' Quoted by Seyyed Hossein Nasr in 'The Cosmos and the Natural Order,' in S.H. Nasr (ed.), *Islamic Spirituality*, vol. 1 Foundations, p. 355, n. 1.

29 'Alī b. Abī Talib, *Dīwān*, ed. 'Abd al-Raḥmān al-Mustāwī (Beirut, 2005), one observes here the seed of the esoteric doctrine later expounded as 'the Perfect Man' (*al-Insān al-kāmil*) in Sufism. It is from such a perspective that the 'microcosmic' mode of interpreting the Qur'ān (known as *taṭbīq*), championed by al-Kāshānī and others, makes perfect sense.

30 *Nahj al-balāgha*, tr. and ed., Ja'far Shahīdī, Sermon 147, p. 143.

31 *Scale of Wisdom*, p. 894.

32 *Scale of Wisdom*, p. 894.

33 Nīsābūrī, *Mustadrak* p. 943, no. 4765. In some versions of this saying, one finds the term 'my progeny (*'itratī*)' instead of 'folk of my household'.

34 Nīsābūrī, *Mustadrak*, p. 927, no. 4685.

35 *Nahj al-balāgha*, tr. and ed., Ja'far Shahīdī, Sermon 133, p. 132.

36 See for the full text of this *ḥadīth* in English and Arabic, *Forty Hadith Qudsi*, tr. E. Ibrahim and D. Johnson-Davies (Beirut and Damascus, 1980), p. 104, no. 38. It is cited there from *Ṣaḥīḥ al-Bukhārī*, *Kitāb al-riqāq*, p. 992, no. 2117; see also Kulaynī, *Uṣūl*, vol. 2, p. 362, for a slightly different variant of this saying.

37 *Scale of Wisdom*, p. 901.

38 *Scale of Wisdom*, p. 895.

39 *Scale of Wisdom*, p. 895.

40 This saying is cited by the contemporary master of Shi'i 'Irfān, Ayatollah Javādī-Āmulī, in his ongoing voluminous commentary on the Qur'ān, *Tasnīm: Tafsīr-i Qur'ān-i karīm* (Qom, 1387 Sh./2008), vol. 1, p. 247. This work promises to be one of the most profound, multi-dimensional and encyclopaedic commentaries in the Muslim exegetical tradition. To date, 13 volumes have been published, and this covers only the first two *Sūra*s of the Qur'ān, and 30 verses of the third. What distinguishes this commentary, apart from its monumental dimensions, is the unique combination of disciplines—both intellectual (*'aqlī*) and transmitted (*naqlī*)—which are used in this commentary: mysticism, theology, philosophy, logic, grammar, lexicography, Ḥadīths, history and other disciplines are creatively and systematically applied to bring to light the multiple levels of meaning and implication of practically each and every verse of the Qur'ān.

41 Javādī-Āmulī, *Tasnīm*, vol. 1, p. 248.

42 Ibn al-ʿArabī, *al-Futūḥāt al-Makkiyya* (Cairo, 1329/1911), vol. 3, p. 94, line 2; as cited by Michel Chodkiewicz, *Un Océan sans rivage: Ibn Arabî, le livre et le loi* (Paris, 1992), p. 47.
43 Martin Lings, *What is Sufism?* (London, 1965), p. 25.
44 *Scale of Wisdom*, p. 897.
45 Cited in al-Qāḍī al-Nuʿmān, *Daʿāʾim al-Islām*, vol. 1, p. 201. The rule pertaining to the recitation of an entire *Sūra* after the *Fātiḥa* is preceded by the words: 'The Imams: They said . . .'.
46 In other words: choose a longer *Sūra* for your prayers.
47 Al-Qāḍī al-Nuʿmān, *Daʿāʾim al-Islām*, p. 192.
48 Al-Qāḍī al-Nuʿmān, *Daʿāʾim al-Islām*, p. 202.

Al-Fātiḥa: The Opening

1 The translations given here are based on that of Pickthall, with certain modifications; the translations of M.A.S. Abdel Haleem (Oxford, 2005) and ʿAlī Qulī Qarāʾī (London, 2004) were also consulted.
2 Cited by Javādī-Āmūlī in *Tasnīm*, vol. 1, p. 262. Javādī-Āmulī notes that this saying is strongly attested by Shiʿi and Sunni sources alike.
3 See Javādī-Āmūlī,*Tasnīm*, vol. 1, pp. 260–266, for these and other epithets.
4 Muḥammad b. Ismāʿīl al-Bukhārī, *Ṣaḥīḥ* (Riyadh, 1994), p. 824, no. 1712.
5 Cited in *Tasnīm*, vol. 1, p. 322.
6 The *Basmala* is an abbreviated reference to the formula *bismi'Llāh al-Raḥmān al-Raḥīm*; just as the word *Tahlīl* abbreviates the testimony *lā ilāha illa'Llāh*; and the *Ḥamdala*, the phrase *al-Ḥamdu li'Llāh,* to cite a few of the other important examples of this kind of abbreviation.
7 See the fascinating commentary on the *Fātiḥa* by the 12th century theologian, Muḥammad b. ʿAbd al-Karīm al-Shahrastānī in Toby Mayer, tr., *Keys to the Arcana: Shahrastānī's Esoteric Commentary on the Qur'an* (Oxford, 2009).
8 Al-Ghazālī refers to the variance in the excellence of the Qurʾānic verses. He refers to the 'light of insight' that helps us to see 'the difference between the Verse of the Throne (2:255) and a verse concerning giving and receiving loans, and between the *Sūra* of Sincerity (112) and the *Sūra* of Destruction (111) . . .' *The Jewels of the Quran*, p. 64. Frithjof Schuon provides a useful image for conveying both the unity of substance and the differentiated qualities of verses within this unity: 'It is necessary to distinguish in the Qurʾān between the general excellence of the Divine Word and the particular excellence of a given content which may be superimposed as, for example, when it is a question of God or of His qualities; it is like the distinction between the excellence of gold and that of some masterpiece made from gold. The masterpiece directly manifests the nobility of gold; similarly the nobility of the content of one or another sacred verse expresses the nobility of the Quranic substance, of the Divine Word, which is in itself undifferentiated; it cannot, however, add to the infinite value of that Word.' F. Schuon, *Understanding Islam* (Bloomington, 1994), p. 46.
9 The ocean is an image often used to convey the limitlessness of meaning in the Qurʾān. For example, Ibn ʿArabī speaks of the Qurʾān as an 'ocean without

a shore' (*al-baḥr alladhī lā sāḥil lahu*), see *al-Futūḥāt al-Makkiyya* (Cairo, 1329/1911), p. 581; as cited in William C. Chittick, *The Sufi Path of Knowledge: Ibn al-ʿArabī and the Metaphysics of the Imagination* (Albany, NY, 1989), p. 245. Michel Chodkiewicz entitles his important work on the hermeneutics of Ibn ʿArabī with this very phrase, *Un Océan Sans Rivage*, as noted above; see p. 55 ff, for discussion of this theme. Martin Lings refers to the Qur'ān as a 'tidal wave' of Revelation flowing from and ebbing to the 'ocean' of infinite reality, and applies this imagery to the *Basmala*: the name *al-Raḥmān*, he writes, 'signifies above all the Ocean Itself in its aspect of Infinite Goodness and Beauty, which by its nature is overflowing; it may therefore, by extension, be taken to signify also the flow of the wave, the Mercy which creates and reveals and sends forth angelic and human Messengers.' The name *al-Raḥīm* 'draws man back to his Origin, enabling him to transcend his human and terrestrial limitations'. M. Lings, *What is Sufism?*, p. 26.

10 This image helps us to see the kind of speculations that have been and can be generated by the idea of the Imam being the 'dot' under the letter *bā'*, and the *bā'* containing everything in the *Basmala*.

11 Some translators of the Qur'ān, such as Muhammad Asad, prefer to use the word 'sustainer' to translate *Rabb*, normally translated as 'Lord'. Asad justifies his use of this word by saying that the term *rabb* 'comprises the ideas of having a just claim to the possession of anything and, consequently, authority over it, a well of rearing, sustaining and fostering anything from its inception to its final completion'. M. Asad, *The Message of the Qur'ān* (Bristol, 2003), vol. 1, p. 5.

12 This verse complements various Prophetic sayings which enjoin meditation on the divine Qualities but not on the divine Essence. Jalāl al-Dīn al-Suyūṭī cites 5 variations on this saying in his compilation of Prophetic sayings, *al-Jāmiʿ al-Ṣaghīr* (Beirut, 1972), vol. 3, pp. 262–263.

13 *Kitāb jāmiʿ al-asrār wa manbaʿ al-anwār*, ed. H. Corbin and O. Yahia (Tehran and Paris, 1969), p. 72. This immensely important figure in the mystical tradition of Shiʿism composed works in which Corbin claims to be able to perceive that form of mystical Shiʿism which is 'conscious of being, in its essence, the esoterism of Islam'. H. Corbin, *En Islam iranien* (Paris, 1971), vol. 2, p. 149.

14 This principle of the 'oneness of being' (*waḥdat al-wujūd*) received its most profound exposition in the corpus of Muḥyī al-Dīn Ibn al-ʿArabī. See Chittick, *Sufi Path*, especially pp. 77–143.

15 The following pages are adapted from the author's essay, 'God "The Loving"' in *A Common Word: Muslims and Christians on Loving God and Neighbour*, ed. Miroslav Volf, Ghazi bin Muhammad, Melissa Yarrington (Grand Rapids and Cambridge, 2010), pp. 88–109; and also from the author's booklet *My Mercy Encompasses All: The Koran's Teachings on Compassion, Peace and Love* (Amory, 2007).

16 Bukhārī, *Ṣaḥīḥ*, p. 954, no. 2014; Sachiko Murata writes that the Sufis, in contrast to the theologians, 'maintain that mercy, love, and gentleness are the overriding reality of existence, and that these will win out in the end. God is not primarily a stern and forbidding father, but a warm and loving mother'. S. Murata, *The Tao of Islam: A Sourcebook on Gender Relationships in Islamic Thought* (Albany, NY, 1992), p. 9.

17 In order to bring home this key aspect of love proper to the root of *raḥma*, the Jewish scholar Ben-Shemesh goes so far as to translate the *Basmala* as 'In the Name of God, the Compassionate, the Beloved.' He argues that in both Arabic and Hebrew the meaning of love is strongly present in the root *r-h-m*, and gives the following evidence: Psalm number 18 contains the phrase: *Erhamha Adonay*—'I love thee my Lord'. See A. Ben Shemesh, 'Some Suggestions to Qur'an Translators', in *Arabica*, 16, 1 (1969), p. 82. In Aramaic/Syriac, the root *r-h-m* specifically denotes love, rather than 'compassion'. One can thus feel the resonance of this Syriac connotation of love within the Arabic word *raḥma*. Moreover, there is epigraphic evidence that early Christian sects in southern Arabic used the name *Rahmanān* as a name of God, and this would probably have been understood as 'The Loving'. See Albert Jamme, 'Inscriptions on the Sabaean Bronze Horse of the Dumbarton Oaks Collection', in *Dumbarton Oaks Papers*, 8 (1954), pp. 323–324 *et passim*.

18 One hundred and thirteen chapters begin with the *Basmala* and only one does not, this exception being *Sūra* 9, *al-Barā'a*, 'Immunity' also known as *al-Tawba*, 'Repentance'. But there are still 114 instances of the phrase in the Qur'ān, as it occurs once in the course of the *Sūrat al-Naml*, 27:30, in the letter addressed by Solomon to the Queen of Sheba.

19 Cited by Bukhārī, Muslim, Nasā'ī and Ibn Mājah; see for both the Arabic and the English translation of the *ḥadīth* in full, E. Ibrahim and D. Johnson-Davies, *Forty Hadith Qudsi*, p. 40. There is another version of this *ḥadīth*, in which the word *sabaqat* ('takes precedence over') is used instead of *taghlibu* ('prevails over'). See, for example, al-Kulaynī, *Uṣūl*, vol. 2, p. 275.

20 E. Ibrahim and D. Johnson-Davies, *Forty Hadith Qudsi*, p. 78 (citing the collections of Bukhārī, Tirmidhī and Ibn Māja).

21 'Every day, He performs a noble work' (*kulla yawmin Huwa fī sha'n*), according to the *Sūrat al-Raḥmān*, 55:29.

22 This is from Jāmī's *Silsilat al-dhahab* as cited by Annemarie Schimmel in her *And Muḥammad is His Messenger* (Chapel Hill and London, 1985), p. 72. She also notes (p. 258) that one of the traditional names of the Prophet is *Rasūl al-raḥma*, 'Prophet of loving mercy'.

23 Louis Massignon notes the extent to which Fāṭima occupies a role in Islam analogous to that of Mary in Christianity, and also refers to the important role she played with regard to the non-Arab Muslims, going so far as describing this role as being the 'inauguration of universal Islam'. He adds: 'The descendants of Fāṭima will henceforth always be the champions of equality, *taswiya*, between non-Arab and Arab believers'. L. Massignon, 'La notion du vœu et la dévotion musulmane à Fâtima', in *Opera Minora*, ed. Y. Moubarac (Paris, 1969), vol. 1, p. 587.

24 See for example, Abu'l-Faḍl (Qāḍī) 'Īyāḍ, *Ash-Shifā'*, *Muḥammad: Messenger of Allāh*, tr. Aisha Abdarrahman Bewley (Inverness, 1991), p. 228.

25 For a revealing evaluation of the cardinal virtue of *ḥilm*, the opposite of which is *jahl* (not simply 'ignorance' but an unwillingness or inability to rein in one's anger, passion and desire), see Toshihiko Izutsu, *God and Man in the Qur'ān: Semantics of the Qur'ānic Weltanschauung* (Kuala Lumpur, 2002), pp. 222–235; and his *Ethico-Religious Concepts in the Qur'an* (Lahore, 2002), pp. 31–34.

26 Qaḍī ʿĪyāḍ, *Ash-Shifā'*, p. 5.
27 ʿAbd al-Razzāq Kāshānī, *Tafsīr Ibn ʿArabī* (Beirut, 2001), vol. 1, p. 7. Kāshānī's commentary is published under the name of Ibn ʿArabī, it being thought that Ibn ʿArabī was the author of this commentary until very recent times.
28 *Tafsīr Ibn ʿArabī*, vol. 2, p. 382.
29 *Tafsīr Ibn ʿArabī*, vol. 2, p. 270.
30 This is found in many traditional compilations. See for example the *Ṣaḥīḥ* of Muslim (Cairo, n.d.), *kitāb al-īmān, bāb maʿrifa ṭarīq al-ru'ya*, p. 94.
31 Cited in *Forty Hadith Qudsi*, p. 126 (referring to the collections of Tirmidhī and Ibn Ḥanbal). One should note here that the Qur'ān refers to the scripture revealed to Moses as being an '*imām*' at 11:17 and 46:12. Conversely, at 36:12, the word '*imām*' is used in the sense of 'book': 'And all things we have recorded in a clear *imām*.'
32 *Ghurar*, vol. 2, p. 1156, no. 1; as cited in Shah-Kazemi, *Justice and Remembrance*, p. 47.
33 Cited in Muḥammad Bāqir Majlisī, *Biḥār al-anwār* (Beirut, 1404/1984), vol. 5, p. 334.
34 See Frithjof Schuon, 'Some Observations on a Problem of the Afterlife', in his *Dimensions of Islam*, tr. Peter Townsend (London, 1970), pp. 136-141, where a compelling argument against the 'eternity' of hell is presented, based partly upon the verses 11:106–7 cited above; and also his excellent critique of Ashʿarite theology, 'Dilemmas of Muslim Scholasticism', in his *Christianity/Islam: Perspectives on Esoteric Ecumenism*, ed. James S. Cutsinger (Bloomington, 2008), pp. 133–168, in which the divine will is shown to be dependent on the divine nature, rather than vice versa.
35 This position is articulated by Kāshānī, in his commentary on Ibn ʿArabī's *Fuṣūṣ al-ḥikam*, and is elucidated by Toshihiko Izutsu, *Sufism and Taoism: A Comparative Study of Key Philosophical Concepts* (Berkeley, Los Angeles, London, 1983), p. 117 ff.
36 We have used here the fine translation of Martin Lings, *The Holy Qur'ān: Translations of Selected Verses* (Cambridge, 2007), p. 188.
37 *Nahj*, p. 449, saying no. 229; as cited in Shah-Kazemi, *Justice and Remembrance*, p. 111.
38 Pickthall wrongly translates *wa'staghfara lahum al-Rasūl* as 'and asked forgiveness of the Messenger', which changes the meaning: God is urging the repentant Muslims to seek the Prophet's prayers for them; they are not seeking the Prophet's forgiveness.
39 This word is often simply translated as 'monotheist', but it means much more than this, or at least, it takes the theological notion of 'monotheism' to its deepest connotation. *Tawḥīd* is the verbal noun of *waḥḥada*, to declare, affirm, and ultimately to realise, oneness; a *muwaḥḥid* is, in esoteric terms, not simply one who as a 'monotheist' declares that there is but one God, but also and essentially, he is one who has *realised* that oneness as such, a realisation predicated upon knowledge of God's all-inclusive oneness (*wāḥidiyya*) and His all-exclusive oneness (*aḥadiyya*). For discussion of this distinction, see Shah-Kazemi, *The Other in the Light of the One*, pp. 76–95.
40 Necessary but not sufficient conditions; they attract but cannot produce that grace by which, alone, salvation is attained, according to basic Islamic theology.

41 A reference to the verse: 'He (Satan) said: My Lord, because Thou hast sent me astray, I verily shall adorn evil for them in the earth, and shall mislead every one of them—except thy purified, sincere slaves' (15:39). We have substantially changed Chittick's rendition of *tazyīn 'adūwī* ('adorning my enemy') given this clear Qur'ānic context: it is the adornment of evil *by the enemy* that the Imam is here referring to.
42 *Supplications: Amīr al-Mu'minīn*, tr. William C. Chittick (London, 1995), verses 43–49 (translation modified).
43 This is from Sermon 1 of the *Nahj al-balāgha*, as cited in Shah-Kazemi, *Justice and Remembrance*, p. 211.
44 *Forty Hadith Qudsi* (translation modified), pp. 85–86, citing this saying from the collections of Muslim, Tirmidhī and Ibn Māja.

Recommended *Sūras*

1 This is reported in most sources, Shi'i and Sunni alike. See for example 'Alī b. Aḥmad al-Wāḥidī, *Asbāb al-nuzūl* (Amman, 2007), on this *Sūra*.
2 One should note that we have here one of the fundamental teachings of the *Bagavad Gita*, referred to there as *nishkama karma*: acting while being detached from the fruits of one's actions. See for further discussion of this theme our reflections on the *Sūrat al-Layl*, 'The Night', no. 92, below.
3 Cited by Sayyid Ḥaydar Āmulī in his Qur'ānic commentary, *al-Muḥīṭ al-a'ẓam* (Qom, 1380 Sh./2001), vol. 1, p. 266. Āmulī cites this saying in reference to 76:5–6, and other verses of the Qur'ān (76:21; 83:25–28, etc.) describing different types of drink given to the believers of different ranks in Paradise.
4 Kāshānī, *Tafsīr*, vol. 2, p. 392.
5 This saying is found in many sources, Sunnī and Shi'i alike. See for example the Qur'ān commentary of Ismā'īl Ḥaqqī Bursevī, *Rūḥ al-bayān*, where he quotes the final part of this saying in his comment on 26:145, vol. 1, p. 297. The English translation given here is from Abū Bakr Sirāj ad-Dīn, *The Book of Certainty* (Cambridge, 1992), p. 75.
6 *Ghurar al-ḥikam*, ed. Mahdī Anṣārī Qummī (Qom, 1380 Sh./2001), p. 177, no. 2537.
7 Cited in Shah-Kazemi, *Justice and Remembrance*, p. 230. The Imam's letter to Mālik is translated here as Appendix 2, pp. 219–236.
8 *Nahj*, p. 475, saying no. 330; as cited in Shah-Kazemi, *Justice and Remembrance*, p. 44.
9 *Nahj*, p. 260; as cited in Shah-Kazemi, *Justice and Remembrance*, p. 116.
10 This is cited in many sources. See, for example, Fakhr al-Din al-Rāzī, *al-Tafsīr al-kabīr* (Beirut, 2001), vol. 3, p. 248.
11 *Nahj*, pp. 196–197; as cited in Shah-Kazemi, *Justice and Remembrance*, p. 57.
12 Quoted by Muḥammad-Jawād Najafī, *Tafsīr-i āsān: Muntakhab az tafāsīr-i mu'tabar* (Tehran, 1359 Sh./1980), at the end of the commentary on the *Sūrat al-A'lā*; Ṭabarsī's *Majma' al-bayān* is cited as the original source.
13 This is attested in nearly all the traditional commentaries on this verse, Sunni and Shi'i alike. See for example Fakhr al-Dīn al-Rāzī, *al-Tafsīr al-kabīr* (Beirut,

2001), vol. 4, p. 383 ff; Abū Jaʿfar al-Ṭabarī, *Jāmiʿ al-bayān* (Beirut, 2001), vol. 6, pp. 343–345.

14 This is widely reported in Sunni and Shiʿi sources. See for example the sources cited by al-Wāḥidī, *Asbāb al-nuzūl*, under 2:274.

15 Kāshānī, *Tafsīr Ibn ʿArabī*, vol. 2, p. 414.

16 William C. Chittick, *Supplications*, p. 40, verse 156 (translation modified).

17 Kāshānī, *Tafsīr Ibn ʿArabī*, vol. 2, p. 447.

18 As cited in the collection *Mukhkh al-ʿibāda* (Beirut, 2008), p. 552; see the excellent English translation of this poem by Shaykh Hamza Yusuf, *The Burda of al-Busiri* (Thaxted, 2002). In his insightful introduction, Shaykh Hamza tells us that this poem 'is arguably the most memorized and recited poem in the Muslim world' (p. xvii).

19 See the discussion of this theme in the Introduction.

20 Cited in Schimmel, *And Muḥammad is His Messenger*, p. 131.

21 In the words of Ibn ʿAṭāʾillāh: 'Remembering God may [also] take the form of a supplication to Him, or the remembrance of His Messengers, Prophets, saints or of anyone related to Him, or close to Him in some way, or because of some deed, such as reciting the Qurʾān, mentioning God's Name, poetry, singing, a conversation or a story.' Ibn ʿAṭāʾillāh al-Iskandarī, *The Key to Salvation: A Sufi Manual of Invocation*, tr. Mary Ann Koury Danner (Cambridge, 1996), p. 45.

22 Cited in Rayshahrī, ed., *Mawsūʿat*, vol. 9, p. 23.

23 Gai Eaton, an eminent and eloquent exponent of Sufism, explains that the reason why this 'shared pattern of belief and behaviour' generates such strong and clearly delineated characters, and does not lead to any 'tedious uniformity' is that Muslims who emulate the Prophet 'have modelled themselves upon a transcendent norm of *inexhaustible richness*'. *Islam and the Destiny of Man* (Cambridge, 1994), p. 187 (emphasis added).

24 2:25. This verse is given as the words uttered by the souls in Paradise upon being given fruits of the heavenly garden.

25 We have slightly modified Arberry's translation of the Qurʾānic verses in this passage. *The Discourses of Rūmī (Fīhi mā fīhi)*, tr. A.J. Arberry (London, 1961), pp. 44–45.

26 One is reminded here of the saying of Wisdom, in the Song of Songs (1:5): 'I am black, but beautiful.' The 'night' of pure receptivity is dark, outwardly, but filled with infinite beauty, inwardly.

27 See the Introduction for discussion of this saying.

28 *Nahj*, p. 414, saying no. 43; as cited in Shah-Kazemi, *Justice and Remembrance*, p. 92.

29 *Nahj*, p. 466, saying no. 281; as cited in Shah-Kazemi, *Justice and Remembrance*, p. 53.

30 The Qurʾān describes those who sold Joseph for a few dirhams as being *zāhidūn* in relation to him (12:20): they deemed him to be worth little.

31 *Ghurar*, ed. Anṣārī, p. 689.

32 *Nahj*, pp. 194–196.

33 Tirmidhī, *Qiyāma*, 26; and Nasāʾī, *Janāʾiz*, 3, as cited in *Al-Ghazālī: The Remembrance of Death and the Afterlife*, tr. T.J. Winter (Cambridge, 1989), p. 9.

34 *Scale of Wisdom*, p. 1206; translation modified.

35 For an English translation of the whole of this dialogue, see William Chittick's *A Shi'ite Anthology* (London, 1980), pp. 38–39.

36 *Ghurar*, vol. 2, p. 1197, no. 18.

37 *Ghurar*, vol. 2, p. 1038, no. 32.

38 Al-Kulaynī, *Uṣūl*, vol. 2, p. 489.

39 For this saying, cited in the collection of Ibn Ḥanbal, and several others of similar import, see the Shaykh al-ʿAlawī's powerful rebuttal of accusations made against the Sufis by 'reformers' in Algeria in the 1920s and 1930s, in Martin Lings, *A Sufi Saint of the Twentieth Century* (London, 1971), pp. 93–95.

40 Makārim Shīrāzī, *Tafsīr-i nimūnah* (Tehran, 1377 Sh./1998), vol. 5, p. 573.

41 Kāshāni, *Tafsīr Ibn ʿArabī*, vol. 2, p. 462.

42 Wāḥidī ascribes these acts to Abū Sufyān. See his *Asbāb al-nuzūl*, under this Sūra entry.

43 *Nahj*, p. 83; as cited in Shah-Kazemi, *Justice and Remembrance*, p. 49.

44 For this range of meanings, see the numerous *ḥadīth*s cited by al-Ṭabarī, *Jāmiʿ al-bayān* (Beirut, 2001), vol. 30, pp. 390–396.

45 Cited in Qaḍī 'Īyāḍ, *Ash-Shifā'*, p. 74.

46 Makārim Shīrāzī, *Tafsīr-i nimūnah*, vol. 5, p. 615; *Tafsīr-i āsān*, vol. 18, p. 400.

47 *Nahj al-balāgha*, ed. Muḥammad ʿAbduh (Beirut, 1996), p. 293.

48 Cited in Shah-Kazemi, *Justice and Remembrance*, p. 220.

49 *Ghurar*, vol. 1, p. 404, no. 3.

50 *Ghurar*, ed. Anṣārī, p. 689, no. 8505.

51 We have gone into this question at length in our *The Other in the Light of the One*, pp. 74–139 and in *Justice and Remembrance*, pp. 161–189.

52 The tenth-century Ismaili philosopher Abū Yaʿqūb al-Sijistānī expresses this apophatic aspect of Imam ʿAlī's perspective on the divine attributes in the opening lines of his work *Kitāb al-yanābīʿ*: 'Praise be to God, hallowed above the attributes of whatever the origination brought into existence, transcending the characteristics of all that speech and hearing embrace, exalted by the mystery of His Unity beyond any comprehending perception, and glorified by the power of His word above all representation in definition or attribute.' Paul E. Walker, tr., *The Wellsprings of Wisdom* (Salt Lake City, 1994), p. 39; as cited by ʿAbd al-Hakeem Carney, 'The Void and the Godhead in Ismailism and Buddhism', in *Sacred Web: A Journal of Tradition and Modernity*, 21 (2008), p. 75.

53 Chittick, *Supplications*, p. 20, verse 6.

54 *Ghurar*, ed. Anṣārī, p. 621, no. 7524.

55 We say 'Christian dogma' and not 'Christian mysticism', as one can find in the corpus of Meister Eckhart (d. 1327), for example, the most exacting conceptions of divine unity. He says in one of his sermons that everything uttered about the Trinity 'is in no way really so or true . . . because every name or in general every thing that denotes a number, or makes a number come to mind, or be conceived, is far from God'. He then quotes a saying from Boethius: 'That is truly one in which there is no number.' The similarity between this and Imam ʿAlī's statement, 'That which has no second does not enter the category of number' is readily apparent. See Bernard McGinn, ed., *Meister Eckhart: Teacher and Preacher* (New Jersey, 1987), pp. 210–211.

56 *Ghurar*, vol. 2, p. 951, no. 9.

Bibliography

ʿAbd al-Bāqī, Fu'ād, ed. *al-Muʿjam al-mufahris li alfāẓ al-Qur'ān al-karīm*. Cairo, 1987.

Abdel Haleem, M.A.S. *The Qur'ān*. Oxford, 2005.

Abū'l-Faḍl (Qāḍī), ʿĪyāḍ. *Ash-Shifā', Muḥammad: Messenger of Allāh*, tr. Aisha Abdarrahman Bewley. Inverness, 1991.

Abul Quasem, M. tr. *The Recitation and Interpretation of the Qur'ān: Al-Ghazālī's Theory*. Kuala Lumpur, 1979.

ʿAlī b. Abī Ṭālib. *Dīwān*, ed. ʿAbd al-Raḥmān al-Muṣṭāwī. Beirut, 2005.

Āmulī, Sayyid Ḥaydar. *Kitāb jāmiʿ al-asrār wa manbaʿ al-anwār*, ed. H. Corbin and O. Yahia. Tehran and Paris, 1969.

—*al-Muḥīṭ al-aʿẓam*. Qom, 1380 Sh./2001.

Arberry, A.J. tr. *The Discourses of Rūmī (Fīhi mā fīhi)*. London, 1961.

Asad, Muhammad. *The Message of the Qur'ān*. Bristol, 2003.

Ben Shemesh, A. 'Some Suggestions to Qur'an Translators', in *Arabica*, 16, 1 (1969), pp. 81–83.

al-Bukhārī, Muḥammad b. Ismāʿīl. *Ṣaḥīḥ*. Riyadh, 1994.

Bursevī, Ismāʿīl Ḥaqqī. *Rūḥ al-bayān*. Istanbul, 1331/1913.

Carney, ʿAbd al-Hakeem. 'The Void and the Godhead in Ismailism and Buddhism', in *Sacred Web: A Journal of Tradition and Modernity*, 21 (2008), pp. 45–93.

Chittick, William C. *A Shiʿite Anthology*. London, 1980.

—*The Sufi Path of Knowledge: Ibn al-ʿArabī and the Metaphysics of the Imagination*. Albany, NY, 1989.

—*Supplications: Amīr al-Mu'minīn*. London, 1995.

Chodkiewicz, Michel. *Un Océan sans rivage: Ibn Arabî, le livre et le loi*. Paris, 1992.

Corbin, Henri. *En Islam iranien*. Paris, 1971.

Eaton, Gai. *Islam and the Destiny of Man*. Cambridge, 1994.

Forty Hadith Qudsi, tr. E. Ibrahim and D. Johnson-Davies. Beirut and Damascus, 1980.

Al-Ghazālī: The Remembrance of Death and the Afterlife, tr. T.J. Winter. Cambridge, 1989.

Ghurar al-ḥikam, ed. Sayyid Ḥusayn Shaykh al-Islāmī. Qom, 2000.

Ghurar al-ḥikam, ed. Mahdī Anṣārī Qummī. Qom, 2001.

Habil, A. 'Traditional Esoteric Commentaries on the Quran', in Seyyed Hossein Nasr, ed., *Islamic Spirituality*, vol. 1, 'Foundations', pp. 24–47.

Ibn al-ʿArabī, Muḥyī al-Dīn. *al-Futūḥāt al-Makkiyya*. Cairo, 1329/1911.

Ibn ʿAṭāʾillāh al-Iskandarī, *The Key to Salvation: A Sufi Manual of Invocation*, tr. Mary Ann Koury Danner. Cambridge, 1996.

Izutsu, Toshihiko. *Sufism and Taoism: A Comparative Study of Key Philosophical Concepts*. Berkeley, CA and London, 1983.

—*Ethico-Religious Concepts in the Qurʾan*. Lahore, 2002.

—*God and Man in the Qurʾān: Semantics of the Qurʾānic Weltanschauung*. Kuala Lumpur, 2002.

Jamme, Albert. 'Inscriptions on the Sabaean Bronze Horse of the Dumbarton Oaks Collection', in *Dumbarton Oaks Papers*, 8 (1954), pp. 317–330.

Javādī-Āmulī, ʿAbd Allāh. *Tasnīm: Tafsīr-i Qurʾān-i karīm*. Qom, 1387 Sh./2008.

Kāshānī, ʿAbd al-Razzāq. *Tafsīr Ibn ʿArabī*. Beirut, 2001.

al-Kulaynī, Muḥammad Yaʿqūb. *al-Uṣūl min al-kāfī*. Tehran, 1376 Sh./1997.

Lings, Martin. *What is Sufism?* London, 1965.

—*A Sufi Saint of the Twentieth Century*. London, 1971.

—*The Holy Qurʾān: Translations of Selected Verses*. Cambridge, 2007.

Majlisī, Muḥammad Bāqir. *Biḥār al-anwār*. Beirut 1404/1984.

Massignon, Louis. 'La notion du voeu et la dévotion musulmane à Fâtima', in *Opera Minora*, ed. Y. Moubarac. Paris, 1969, vol. 1, pp. 573–591.

Mawsūʿat al-Imām ʿAlī ibn Abī Ṭālib fiʾl-kitāb waʾl-sunna waʾl-taʾrīkh, ed. Muḥammad Rayshahrī. Qom, 1421/2000.

McGinn, Bernard, ed. *Meister Eckhart: Teacher and Preacher*. New Jersey, 1987.

Mukhkh al-ʿibāda. Beirut, 2008.

Murādī, Muḥammad, 'Rawish-i tafsīr-i Qurʾān' in ʿAlī-Akbar Rashād, ed., *Dānish-nāmah-i Imām ʿAlī*. Tehran, 2001, vol. 1, pp. 229–284.

Murata, Sachiko. *The Tao of Islam: A Sourcebook on Gender Relationships in Islamic Thought*. Albany, NY, 1992.

Muslim, b. al-Ḥajjāj. *Ṣaḥīḥ*. Cairo, n.d.

Nasr, Seyyed Hossein. 'The Cosmos and the Natural Order,' in S.H. Nasr, ed., *Islamic Spirituality*, vol. 1, 'Foundations'. London, 1987, pp. 345–357.

—'Islam', in Arvind Sharma, ed., *Our Religions*, pp. 425–532. San Francisco, 1993.

Nahj al-balāgha, ed. Shaykh ʿAzīzullāh al-ʿUṭāridī. Tehran, 1993.

Nahj al-balāgha, ed. Muḥammad ʿAbduh. Beirut, 1996.

Nahj al-balāgha, ed. and tr. Jaʿfar Shahīdi. Tehran, 1378 Sh./1999.

Najafī, Muḥammad-Jawād. *Tafsīr-i āsān: Muntakhab az tafāsīr-i muʿtabar*. Tehran, 1359 Sh./1980.

al-Nīsābūrī, al-Ḥākim. *al-Mustadrak ʿalaʾl-ṣaḥīḥayn*. Beirut, 2002.

al-Nuʿmān b. Muḥammad, al-Qāḍī Abū Ḥanīfa. *Daʿāʾim al-Islām*, tr. Asaf A.A. Fyzee, revised by I.K. Poonawala, as *The Pillars of Islam*. New Delhi, 2002–2004.

Pickthall, M.M. *The Glorious Koran*. London, 1976.
Qulī Qarā'ī. *The Qur'ān*. London, 2004.
al-Rāzī, Fakhr al-Dīn. *al-Tafsīr al-kabīr*. Beirut, 2001.
Rosenthal, Franz. *Knowledge Triumphant: The Concept of Knowledge in Medieval Islam*. Leiden and Boston, 2007.
The Scale of Wisdom: A Compendium of Shi'a Hadith, ed. N. Virjee. London, 2009.
Schimmel, Annemarie. *And Muḥammad is His Messenger*. Chapel Hill and London, 1985.
Schuon, Frithjof. *Dimensions of Islam*. London, 1970.
—*Understanding Islam*. Bloomington, 1994.
—*Christianity/Islam: Perspectives on Esoteric Ecumenism*. Bloomington, 2008.
Sells, Michael. 'A Literary Approach to the Hymnic Sūras of the Qur'ān', in Issa Boullata, ed., *Literary Structures of Religious Meaning in the Qur'ān*. Richmond, 2000, pp. 3–25.
Shah-Kazemi, Reza. *Justice and Remembrance: Introducing the Spirituality of Imam 'Alī*. London, 2006.
—*The Other in the Light of the One: The Universality of the Qur'an and Interfaith Dialogue*. Cambridge, 2006.
—*My Mercy Encompasses All: The Koran's Teachings on Compassion, Peace and Love*. Amory, 2007.
—'God "The Loving"' in Miroslav Volf, Ghazi bin Muhamma and Melissa Yarrington, ed., *A Common Word: Muslims and Christians on Loving God and Neighbour*. Grand Rapids and Cambridge, 2010, pp. 88–109.
al-Shahrastānī, Muḥammad b. 'Abd al-Karīm. *Mafātīḥ al-asrār*, tr. Toby Mayer as *Keys to the Arcana: Shahrastānī's Esoteric Commentary on the Qur'an*. Oxford, 2009.
Shīrāzī, Makārim. *Tafsīr-i nimūnah*. Tehran, 1377 Sh./1998.
Al-Sijistānī, Abū Ya'qūb. *Kitāb al-yanābī'*, tr. Paul Walker as *The Wellsprings of Wisdom*. Salt Lake City, 1994.
Sirāj ad-Dīn, Abū Bakr. *The Book of Certainty*. Cambridge, 1992.
al-Suyūṭī, Jalāl al-Dīn. *al-Jāmi' al-ṣaghīr*. Beirut, 1972.
al-Ṭabarī, Abū Ja'far Muḥammad b. Jarīr. *Jāmi' al-bayān*. Beirut, 2001.
al-Wāḥidī, 'Alī b. Aḥmad. *Asbāb al-nuzūl*. Amman, 2007.
Yusuf, Hamza. *The Burda of al-Busiri*. Thaxted, 2002.